First World War
and Army of Occupation
War Diary
France, Belgium and Germany

49 DIVISION
147 Infantry Brigade,
Brigade Machine Gun Company
26 January 1916 - 27 February 1918

WO95/2802/2

The Naval & Military Press Ltd
www.nmarchive.com
Published in association with The National Archives

Published by

The Naval & Military Press Ltd

Unit 10 Ridgewood Industrial Park,

Uckfield, East Sussex,

TN22 5QE England

Tel: +44 (0) 1825 749494

www.naval-military-press.com

www.nmarchive.com

Contents

Document type	Place/Title	Date From	Date To
Heading	WO95/2802 147 Bde 47 Div Bde MGC Feb'16-Feb'18		
Heading	49th Division 147th Infy Bde 147th Bde Mach Gun Coy. Feb 1916-Feb 1918		
Heading	War Diary Of 147th Bde Machine Gun Coy. From Jan 26 1916 To April 30th 1916 Vol 18		
Miscellaneous	A.G. Office Base	12/05/1916	12/05/1916
War Diary	Wormhoudt	26/01/1916	03/02/1916
War Diary	Esquelbec	03/02/1916	03/02/1916
War Diary	Longeau	04/02/1916	04/02/1916
War Diary	Molliens Vidame	05/02/1916	11/02/1916
War Diary	Ailly Sur Somme	12/02/1916	12/02/1916
War Diary	Mirvaux	13/02/1916	13/02/1916
War Diary	Bouzincourt	14/02/1916	27/02/1916
War Diary	Hedauville	28/02/1916	07/03/1916
War Diary	Bertrancourt	08/03/1916	28/03/1916
War Diary	Talmas	29/03/1916	29/03/1916
War Diary	La Yicogne	29/03/1916	04/04/1916
War Diary	Naours	05/04/1916	30/04/1916
Heading	War Diary 147th Bde M.G. Coy. From 1/5/16 To 31/5/16 Volume		
War Diary	Naours	01/05/1916	31/05/1916
Heading	147th Brigade. 49th Division 147th Brigade Machine Gun Company June 1916		
War Diary	Rubempre	01/06/1916	01/06/1916
War Diary	Martinsart	02/06/1916	11/06/1916
War Diary	Forceville	11/06/1916	23/06/1916
War Diary	Contay	23/06/1916	27/06/1916
War Diary	Senlis	28/06/1916	28/06/1916
War Diary	Vadencourt	29/06/1916	30/06/1916
Heading	147th Inf. Bde. 49th Div. War Diary 147th Machine Gun Company July 1916		
War Diary	Aveluy Wood	01/07/1916	01/07/1916
War Diary	Crucifix Dugouts	02/07/1916	02/07/1916
War Diary	Thiepval Wood	03/07/1916	07/07/1916
War Diary	Aveluy Wood	08/07/1916	09/07/1916
War Diary	Thiepval Wood	10/07/1916	30/07/1916
Heading	147th Brigade. 49th Division 147th Brigade Machine Gun Company August 1916		
Miscellaneous	D.A.G. 3rd Echelon		
War Diary	Thiepval Wood	01/08/1916	14/08/1916
War Diary	Arqueves	25/08/1916	27/08/1916
War Diary	Forceville	27/08/1916	29/08/1916
War Diary	Thiepval Wood	29/08/1916	31/08/1916
War Diary	Thiepval Wood	15/08/1916	21/08/1916
War Diary	Arqueves	22/08/1916	24/08/1916
Heading	147th. Infantry Brigade 49th. Division 147th. Machine Gun Company September 1916		
Miscellaneous	D.A.G. 3rd Echelon		
War Diary	Thiepval Wood	01/09/1916	04/09/1916
War Diary	Hedauville	05/09/1916	16/09/1916

War Diary	Authville Wood	16/09/1916	24/09/1916
War Diary	Aveluy & Ovillers	25/09/1916	26/09/1916
War Diary	Aveluy	27/09/1916	28/09/1916
War Diary	Gaudiempre	29/09/1916	30/09/1916
Miscellaneous	14th Inf Bn.	03/10/1916	03/10/1916
War Diary	Bienvillers	01/10/1916	20/10/1916
War Diary	Fonquevillers	21/10/1916	31/10/1916
Heading	War Diary Of 147th M.G. Corps For November 1916 Vol XI		
War Diary	Fonquevillers	01/11/1916	30/11/1916
Heading	War Diary Of 147 Machine Gun Coy From 1-12-16 To 31.12.16. Vol 12		
War Diary	Fonquevillers	01/12/1916	08/12/1916
War Diary	Causmesnil	09/12/1916	31/12/1916
Heading	War Diary 147 Machine Gun Coy. From 1.1.17 To 31.1.17 Vol 13		
War Diary	Causmesnil	01/01/1917	07/01/1917
War Diary	Berles Au Bois	08/01/1917	31/01/1917
Miscellaneous			
Map	Edition 2. C Trenches Corrected to 22-6-26 Sheet 51c S.E.		
Miscellaneous	Glossary		
Heading	War Diary 149 Machine Gun Coy From 1.2.17 To 28.2.17 Volume 14		
War Diary	Bellacourt	01/02/1917	01/02/1917
War Diary	Riviere	02/02/1917	28/02/1917
Heading	War Diary Of 147 Machine Gun Company From 1/3/17 To 31/3/17 Vol. 15		
War Diary	Riviere	01/03/1917	01/03/1917
War Diary	Bailleulval	02/03/1917	02/03/1917
War Diary	Grenas	03/03/1917	06/03/1917
War Diary	Bouquemaison	07/03/1917	07/03/1917
War Diary	Doullens	08/03/1917	08/03/1917
War Diary	Vieille Chapelle	09/03/1917	09/03/1917
War Diary	Richebourg	09/03/1917	31/03/1917
Heading	War Diary Of The 147th Machine Gun Company From 1-4-17 To 30-4-17 Vol 16		
War Diary	Richebourg	01/04/1917	05/04/1917
War Diary	Vieille Chapelle	06/04/1917	19/04/1917
War Diary	Richebourg	20/04/1917	30/04/1917
Heading	War Diary Of 147th Machine Gun Coy From 1.5.17 To 31.5.17 Vol 17		
War Diary	Richebourg	01/05/1917	31/05/1917
Heading	War Diary 147th Machine Gun Company 30th June 1917 Vol. 18		
War Diary	Ferme Du Bois Sector Richebourg	01/06/1917	14/06/1917
War Diary	Ferme Du Bois	15/06/1917	16/06/1917
War Diary	Zelobes	17/06/1917	17/06/1917
War Diary	Zelobes & Noyelles	18/06/1917	18/06/1917
War Diary	St Elie Sector Loos	19/06/1917	29/06/1917
War Diary	Noyelles	30/06/1917	30/06/1917
Heading	147th Machine Gun Company War Diary For July 1917 Vol 19		
Heading	147th Machine Gun Company War Diary For July 1917.		
War Diary	Noyelles	01/07/1917	01/07/1917

War Diary	Bethune	02/07/1917	02/07/1917
War Diary	Regnier Le Clere	03/07/1917	13/07/1917
War Diary	Dunkirk	14/07/1917	17/07/1917
War Diary	Bray Dunes	18/07/1917	19/07/1917
War Diary	Ghyvelde	20/07/1917	31/07/1917
Heading	147th Machine Gun Company War Diary For August 1917 Vol 20		
War Diary	Ghyvelde	31/07/1917	31/07/1917
War Diary	Hd Qrs Ghyvelde	02/08/1917	02/08/1917
War Diary	Hd Quarters Bray Dunes	03/08/1917	11/08/1917
War Diary	Oust Dunkirk	12/08/1917	14/08/1917
War Diary	Coast Defences Nieuport Bains St. Idesbalde	15/08/1917	30/08/1917
Operation(al) Order(s)	147th Machine Gun Company Operation Orders No. 1	13/08/1917	13/08/1917
Operation(al) Order(s)	147th Machine Gun Company Operation Orders No. 2	19/08/1917	19/08/1917
Operation(al) Order(s)	147th Machine Gun Company Operation Orders No. 3	26/08/1917	26/08/1917
Heading	War Diary Of 147 Machine Gun Coy For September 1917 Vol 21		
Heading	War Diary Of 147th Machine Gun Coy Dated 01/09/1917 To 30/09/1917		
War Diary	Coast Defences Nieuport Bains St. Idesbalde	31/08/1917	06/09/1917
War Diary	Coast Defences Nieuport Bains To La Panne	07/09/1917	16/09/1917
War Diary	Ghyvelde	17/09/1917	23/09/1917
War Diary	Teteghem	23/09/1917	25/09/1917
War Diary	Buysscheure	25/09/1917	27/09/1917
War Diary	Westbecourt	28/09/1917	28/09/1917
War Diary	Esquerdes	29/09/1917	29/09/1917
War Diary	Staples	30/09/1917	30/09/1917
Operation(al) Order(s)	147th Machine Gun Company Operation Orders No. 8	22/09/1917	22/09/1917
Operation(al) Order(s)	147th Machine Gun Company Operation Orders No. 7	16/09/1917	16/09/1917
Operation(al) Order(s)	147th Machine Gun Company Operation Orders No. 10	24/09/1917	24/09/1917
Operation(al) Order(s)	147th Machine Gun Company Operation Orders No. 9	23/09/1917	23/09/1917
Operation(al) Order(s)	147th Machine Gun Company Operation Orders No. 6	14/09/1917	14/09/1917
Operation(al) Order(s)	147th Machine Gun Company Operation Orders No. 4	02/09/1917	02/09/1917
Heading	War Diary Of 147 Machine Gun Coy For 1st To 31st October 1917 Vol 22		
War Diary	Staples	01/10/1917	01/10/1917
War Diary	Staple	02/10/1917	02/10/1917
War Diary	Abeele	03/10/1917	03/10/1917
War Diary	Nr. Vlamatinge	04/10/1917	05/10/1917
War Diary	Zonnebeke Sector	06/10/1917	09/10/1917
War Diary	W of Passhendaele	09/10/1917	10/10/1917
War Diary	X Camp St Jean	11/10/1917	15/10/1917
War Diary	Vlamatinge Area 3	16/10/1917	24/10/1917
War Diary	Winnezeele	25/10/1917	27/10/1917
War Diary	Steenvoorde	28/10/1917	30/10/1917
Heading	War Diary Of 147th Mach Gun Coy For November 1917 Vol 23		
War Diary	Steenvorde	31/10/1917	09/11/1917
War Diary	Canal Area	10/11/1917	23/11/1917
War Diary	Trenches Becelaere Sector	24/11/1917	29/11/1917
Heading	War Diary Of 147th Machine Gun Company For Month Of December 1917 Vol 24		
War Diary	Trenches Becelaere Sector	30/11/1917	06/12/1917
War Diary	Reserve Billets Dickebusch Area	07/12/1917	11/12/1917
War Diary	Rest Billets Dickebush Area	12/12/1917	12/12/1917
War Diary	Zonnebeke Area	13/12/1917	20/12/1917

War Diary	Reserve Billets Belgium Battery Corner	21/12/1917	22/12/1917
War Diary	Zonnebeke Sector	23/12/1917	30/12/1917
Heading	War Diary Of 147 Mach Gun Coy For January 18 Vol 25		
Miscellaneous	147 Inf: Bgd	31/01/1918	31/01/1918
War Diary	Zonnebeke Sector	31/12/1917	08/01/1918
War Diary	St Marie Cappel Area	09/01/1918	10/01/1918
War Diary	Caestre Area	11/01/1918	30/01/1918
Heading	War Diary Of 147 Mach Gun Coy for February 1918 Vol 26		
War Diary	Caestre Area	31/01/1918	20/02/1918
War Diary	Forward Area	21/02/1918	27/02/1918

WO95/2802 (2)

147 BDE 49 DIV

BDE MGC

Feb '16 – Feb '18

49TH DIVISION

147TH INFY BDE

147TH BDE MACH. GUN COY.

FEB 1916-FEB 1918

49
Vol 1.2
3 & 4

CONFIDENTIAL

WAR DIARY

OF

147TH BDE. MACHINE GUN COY.

FROM. JAN 26 . 1916 TO. APRIL 30TH 1916

/

Feb '18

VOLUME I to 4 1.2.3.4.

A/131.

A.G.s Office
Base

Herewith we enclose
WAR DIARY of the 147th Bde
M. G. Coy. from 26 January 1916
to April 30th 1916

12/5/16

W. J. McSpurrle [?]
Capt.
147 Bde. Machine Gun Coy.

Army Form C. 2118.

Instructions regarding War Diaries and Intelligence Summaries are contained in F. S. Regs., Part II. and the Staff Manual respectively. Title Pages will be prepared in manuscript.

WAR DIARY
or
~~INTELLIGENCE SUMMARY~~
(Erase heading not required.)

Place	Date	Hour	Summary of Events and Information	Remarks and references to Appendices
Wormhoudt	26/1/16		Formation of the 147th Bde M. G. Coy.	
	27/1/16		Company Training.	
	28/1/16		As for 27/1/16	
	29/1/16		As for 27/1/16	
	30/1/16		Ordinary Routine.	
	31/1/16		As for 30/1/16	
	1/2/16		As for 30/1/16.	
	2/2/16		As for 30/1/16	
	3/2/16		Preparing to move.	
		6 P.M.	Left Wormhoudt	
			When nearing Esquelbec a light railway engine ran into & overturned G.S. wagon & water cart. Two men sustained minor injuries.	
Esquelbec		8 P.M.	Entrained	

[illegible]

2449 Wt. W14957/M90 750,000 1/16 J.B.C. & A. Forms/C.2118/12.

Army Form C. 2118.

WAR DIARY
or
~~INTELLIGENCE SUMMARY~~

(Erase heading not required.)

Instructions regarding War Diaries and Intelligence Summaries are contained in F. S. Regs., Part II. and the Staff Manual respectively. Title Pages will be prepared in manuscript.

Place	Date	Hour	Summary of Events and Information	Remarks and references to Appendices
LONGEAU.	4/2/16.	10 a.m.	After travelling all night arrived at Longeau & marched through Amiens forward to Ailly-sur-Somme & we conveyed by buses to MOLLIENS VIDAME.	
MOLLIENS VIDAME.	5/2/16.		Company Training.	
"	6/2/16		As for 5/2/16	
"	7/2/16		As for 5/2/16	
"	8/2/16		As for 5/2/16	
"	9/2/16		As for 5/2/16	
"	10/2/16		As for 5/2/16	
"	11/2/16	8 A.M.	Left MOLLIENS VIDAME & marched to AILLY SUR SOMME VIA FLOXICOURT & BRIQUESMENIL.	
AILLY-SUR SOMME.	12/2/16.	6.45 A.M.	Marched from AILLY SUR SOMME TO MIRVAUX VIA ST SAUVEUR BERTANGLES, VILLERS BOCAGE & MOLLIENS AU-BOIS.	

[illegible signature]

2449 Wt. W14957/M90 750,000 1/16 J.B.C. & A. Forms/C.2118/12.

Instructions regarding War Diaries and Intelligence Summaries are contained in F. S. Regs., Part II. and the Staff Manual respectively. Title Pages will be prepared in manuscript.

WAR DIARY

or

~~INTELLIGENCE SUMMARY~~

(Erase heading not required.)

Army Form C. 2118.

Place	Date	Hour	Summary of Events and Information	Remarks and references to Appendices
MIRVAUX	[illegible]/2/16	1.45 P.M.	Marched from Mirvaux to BOUZINCOURT via RUBEMPRE, HERISSART WARLOY, BAILLEUL & SENLIS	
BOUZINCOURT	14/2/16		Company Training	
	15/2/16		As for 14/2/16.	
	16/2/16		As for 14/2/16	
	17/2/16		As for 14/2/16	
	[illegible]/2/16		As for 14/2/16	
	[illegible]/2/16		As for 14/2/16	
	[illegible]/2/16		As for 14/2/16	
	21/2/16		As for 14/2/16	
	22/2/16		As for 14/2/16	
	23/2/16		As for 14/2/16	
	24/2/16		As for 14/2/16	

[illegible]

2449 Wt. W14957/M90 750,000 1/16 J.B.C. & A. Forms/C.2118/12.

Army Form C. 2118.

Instructions regarding War Diaries and Intelligence Summaries are contained in F. S. Regs., Part II. and the Staff Manual respectively. Title Pages will be prepared in manuscript.

WAR DIARY
or
~~INTELLIGENCE SUMMARY~~

(Erase heading not required.)

Place	Date	Hour	Summary of Events and Information	Remarks and references to Appendices
BOUZINCOURT	25/2/16		As for 24/2/16	
"	26/2/16		As for 24/2/16	
"	27/2/16	3am	Headquarters & No 3 Section left Bouzincourt for Hedauville.	
		6am	Nos 1, 2 & 4 Sections left BOUZINCOURT to occupy trenches	
			Nos 2 & 4 Sections in first line trenches to right of Thiepval	
			No 1 Section in the Authuille defences.	
HEDAUVILLE	28/2/16		Headquarters & No 3 Section	
			Nos 1, 2 & 4 Sections as for 27/2/16	
"	29/2/16		As for 28/2/16	
	1/3/16		As for 28/2/16	
	2/3/16		As for 1/3/16	
	3/3/16		Hqrs & No 4 Section at Hedauville	
			No 1 Section in Right Sector	
			No 2 Section in AUTHUILLE defences	
			No 3 Section in Left Sector.	

2449 Wt. W14957/M90 750,000 1/16 J.B.C. & A. Forms/C.2118/12.

Army Form C. 2118.

Instructions regarding War Diaries and Intelligence Summaries are contained in F. S. Regs., Part II. and the Staff Manual respectively. Title Pages will be prepared in manuscript.

WAR DIARY
or
~~INTELLIGENCE SUMMARY~~
(Erase heading not required.)

Place	Date	Hour	Summary of Events and Information	Remarks and references to Appendices
HEDAUVILLE	4/3/16		As for 3/3/16	
"	5/3/16		As for 3/3/16	
"	6/3/16		As for 3/3/16	
"	7/3/16	2 am	Headquarters & No 4 Section left HEDAUVILLE for BERTRANCOURT via FORCEVILLE.	
			Nos 1 2 & 3 Sections withdraw M. Guns from trenches	
BERTRANCOURT	8/3/16	1 am	Nos 1 2 & 3 Sections occupy new billets at Bertrancourt after leaving trenches on preceding day at 8 pm & marching via BOUZINCOURT, HEDAUVILLE, FORCEVILLE.	
"	9/3/16		Company Training	
"	10/3/16		As for 9/3/16	
	11/3/16		As for 9/3/16	
"	12/3/16		Rest Billets Church Parade	
"	13/3/16		Company Training	
	14/3/16		As for 13/3/16	

2449 Wt. W14957/M90 750,000 1/16 J.B.C. & A. Forms/C.2118/12.

Army Form C. 2118.

WAR DIARY
or
~~INTELLIGENCE SUMMARY~~

(Erase heading not required.)

Instructions regarding War Diaries and Intelligence Summaries are contained in F. S. Regs., Part II. and the Staff Manual respectively. Title Pages will be prepared in manuscript.

Place	Date	Hour	Summary of Events and Information	Remarks and references to Appendices
BERTRANCOURT	15/3/16		As for 13/3/16	
"	16/3/16		As for 13/3/16	
"	17/3/16		As for 13/3/16	
"	18/3/16		As for 13/3/16	
"	19/3/16		Rest Billets. Church Parade.	
"	20/3/16		Company Training.	
"	21/3/16		As for 20/3/16	
"	22/3/16		As for 20/3/16	
"	23/3/16		As for 20/3/16	
"	24/3/16		As for 20/3/16	
"	25/3/16		As for 20/3/16	
"	26/3/16		Rest Billets. Church Parade	
"	27/3/16		Company Training.	
"	28/3/16	7.45 a.m.	Left BERTRANCOURT AT 7.45 A.M. for TALMAS Via ACHEUX, LEALVILLERS, TOUTENCOURT & HERISSART.	
		2.30 p.m.	Arrived at TALMAS & took over rest billets.	

[illegible signature]

2449 Wt. W14957/M90 750,000 1/16 J.B.C. & A. Forms/C.2118/12.

Instructions regarding War Diaries and Intelligence Summaries are contained in F. S. Regs., Part II. and the Staff Manual respectively. Title Pages will be prepared in manuscript.

WAR DIARY
or
~~INTELLIGENCE SUMMARY~~
(Erase heading not required.)

Army Form C. 2118.

Place	Date	Hour	Summary of Events and Information	Remarks and references to Appendices
TALMAS	29/3/16	2 PM	Moved from rest billets in TALMAS to LA VICOGNE	
LA VICOGNE	29/3/16	3 P.M.	Arrived at LA VICOGNE & took over rest billets	
"	30/3/16		In rest billets. Company Training	
"	31/3/16		In rest billets Company Training	
"	1/4/16		In rest billets Company Training	
"	2/4/16		In rest billets Company Training	
"	3/4/16		In rest billets Company Training	
"	4/4/16	2 PM	Moved from LA VICOGNE & took over billets at NAOURS	
NAOURS	5/4/16		In rest billets Company Training	
"	6/4/16		In rest billets. Company Training.	
"	7/4/16.		In rest billets. Company Training	
	8/4/16		Training in Anti Gas Appliances under 2/Lieut. Stott. 49th Divisional Gas School. & Company Training as usual.	

2449 Wt. W14957/M90 750,000 1/16 J.B.C. & A. Forms/C.2118/12.

Instructions regarding War Diaries and Intelligence Summaries are contained in F. S. Regs., Part II. and the Staff Manual respectively. Title Pages will be prepared in manuscript.

WAR DIARY

or

~~INTELLIGENCE SUMMARY~~

(Erase heading not required.)

Army Form C. 2118.

Place	Date	Hour	Summary of Events and Information	Remarks and references to Appendices
NAOURS	9/4/16		As for 8/4/16.	
"	10/4/16		As for 8/4/16	
"	11/4/16		As for 8/4/16.	
"	12/4/16		Company Training as usual.	
"	13/4/16		As for 12/4/16	
"	14/4/16		As for 12/4/16	
"	15/4/16		As for 12/4/16.	
"	16/4/16		Rest billets Church Parade.	
"	17/4/16		Company Training as usual.	
"	18/4/16		As for 17/4/16	
"	19/4/16		As for 17/4/16	
"	20/4/16		As for 17/4/16	
"	21/4/16		As for 17/4/16	
"	22/4/16		As for 17/4/16	
"	23/4/16		Rest billets Church Parade	
"	24/4/16		Company training as usual.	

[illegible signature]

2449 Wt. W14957/M90 750,000 1/16 J.B.C. & A. Forms/C.2118/12.

Instructions regarding War Diaries and Intelligence Summaries are contained in F. S. Regs., Part II. and the Staff Manual respectively. Title Pages will be prepared in manuscript.

WAR DIARY
or
~~INTELLIGENCE SUMMARY~~

(Erase heading not required.)

Army Form C. 2118.

Place	Date	Hour	Summary of Events and Information	Remarks and references to Appendices
NAOURS.	25/4/16		Company Training as usual.	
"	26/4/16		As for 25/4/16.	
	27/4/16		As for 25/4/16.	
		1 A.M.	Fire broke out in 147/1 T.M. Battery's billet caused by explosion of Trench Mortar Bombs. The 147th Bde M.G. Coys Officers Mess was badly damaged by fire. Several of the inhabitants of the houses in question & those in the immediate vicinity were severely burnt or wounded by splinters caused by the explosion of the bombs. Two T.M.B men were wounded & also one man of the Bde M.G. Coy. The fire raged fiercely for 15 hours when the local fire brigade assisted by the other troops billeted in the village gained the upper hand.	
"	28/4/16		Ruins of fire still smouldering. Small outbreaks of fire occurring. Company Training as usual.	
"	29/4/16		Field Day of the 147th Inf Bde. Practice Attack.	
"	30/4/16		Rest billets Church Parade	

2449 Wt. W14957/M90 750,000 1/16 J.B.C. & A. Forms/C.2118/12.

49

Vol 5

— CONFIDENTIAL —

WAR DIARY

147th Bde. M. G. Coy.

FROM 1/5/16 TO 31/5/16

VOLUME ____

Army Form C. 2118.

WAR DIARY
or
INTELLIGENCE SUMMARY

(Erase heading not required.)

Instructions regarding War Diaries and Intelligence Summaries are contained in F. S. Regs., Part II. and the Staff Manual respectively. Title Pages will be prepared in manuscript.

Place	Date	Hour	Summary of Events and Information	Remarks and references to Appendices
NAOURS.	1/5/16		Company Training as usual	
"	2/5/16		As for 1/5/16	
"	3/5/16		Field Day of the 147th Bde. Owing to heavy rains the scheme of the "ATTACK" was abandoned.	
"	4/5/16		Company Training as usual	
"	5/5/16		Field Day of the 147th & 148th Inf. Bdes. Practice "ATTACK"	
"	6/5/16		Company Training as usual.	
"	7/5/16		Rest in Billets. Church Parade.	
"	8/5/16		Company Training as usual	
"	9/5/16		As for 8/5/16	
"	10/5/16		As for 8/5/16	
"	11/5/16		As for 9/5/16 Showery.	
"	12/5/16		Company Training. Weather fine. Nothing to report	
"	13/5/16		Company Training. Heavy Showers of rain	
"	14/5/16		Company Training. Weather fine. Nothing further to report.	

[illegible]

2449 Wt. W14957/M90 750,000 1/16 J.B.C. & A. Forms/C.2118/12.

Army Form C. 2118.

Instructions regarding War Diaries and Intelligence Summaries are contained in F. S. Regs., Part II. and the Staff Manual respectively. Title Pages will be prepared in manuscript.

WAR DIARY
or
INTELLIGENCE SUMMARY
(Erase heading not required.)

Place	Date	Hour	Summary of Events and Information	Remarks and references to Appendices
NAOURS	15/5/16		Company Training as usual. Heavy showers of rain. Fine during afternoon.	
"	16/5/16		Field Day of the 49th Division. Tactical Scheme. Weather Fine.	
"	17/5/16		Company Training as usual. Weather Fine. Nothing further to report. 1st day of Divisional Horse Show. 1 pr light draught horses selected in first four.	
"	18/5/16		Company Training as usual. Weather Fine. Awarded 1st prize in Class 16 for Light Draught Horses at Divisional Horse Show.	
"	19/5/16		Company Training as usual. Weather Fine.	
"	20/5/16		As for 19/5/16.	
"	21/5/16		Church Parade. Rest Billets.	
"	22/5/16		Company Training as usual.	
"	23/5/16		As for 22/5/16	
"	24/5/16		As for 22/5/16.	
"	25/5/16		As for 22/5/16	

[illegible initials]

2449 Wt. W14957/M90 750,000 1/16 J.B.C. & A. Forms/C.2118/12.

Instructions regarding War Diaries and Intelligence Summaries are contained in F. S. Regs., Part II. and the Staff Manual respectively. Title Pages will be prepared in manuscript.

WAR DIARY
or
INTELLIGENCE SUMMARY

(Erase heading not required.)

Army Form C. 2118.

Place	Date	Hour	Summary of Events and Information	Remarks and references to Appendices
NAOURS	26/5/16		Company Training as usual.	
"	27/5/16		As for 26/5/16	
"	28/5/16		As for 26/5/16 Church Parade.	
"	29/5/16		Company Training. Inter section Competitions.	
	30/5/16		Company Training. Received Operation Orders to prepare to move.	
	31/5/16		Left NAOURS at 2.30pm & proceed via TALMAS to RUBEMPRE.	

2449 Wt. W14957/M90 750,000 1/16 J.B.C. & A. Forms/C.2118/12.

147th Brigade.

49th Divisogn.

147th BRIGADE MACHINE GUN COMPANY

J U N E 1 9 1 6

49

Instructions regarding War Diaries and Intelligence Summaries are contained in F. S. Regs., Part II. and the Staff Manual respectively. Title pages will be prepared in manuscript.

WAR DIARY
or
~~INTELLIGENCE SUMMARY.~~
(Erase heading not required.)

Army Form C. 2118.

147 Bde M G Coy
Vol 6

Place	Date	Hour	Summary of Events and Information	Remarks and references to Appendices
RUBEMPRE.	1/6/16	6AM	Left RUBEMPRE for MARTINSART, Via HERISSART, CONTAY, VADENCOURT, WARLOY-BAILLON, SENLIS & BOUZINCOURT. Transport Lines at HEDAUVILLE.	
MARTINSART.	2/6/16	.	Company Training. Weather Fine. Supporting Brigade to 36th Division.	
"	3/6/16		As for 2/6/16 Weather Fine	
"	4/6/16		As for 2/6/16.	
"	5/6/16		As for 2/6/16	
	6/6/16		Company Training. Heavy Rains. Nothing further to report.	
	7/6/16		Company Training.	
	8/6/16		As for 7/6/16.	
	9/6/16		As for 7/6/16.	
	10/6/16		As for 7/6/16	
	11/6/16		Moved from MARTINSART to FORCEVILLE at 4.00pm Via ENGELBELMER.	
FORCEVILLE.	11/6/16		Very heavy rains.	
	12/6/16		Company Training as usual. Raining most of the day.	

G.C.P.

T2134. Wt. W708—776. 500000. 4/15. Sir J. C. & S.

Instructions regarding War Diaries and Intelligence Summaries are contained in F. S. Regs., Part II. and the Staff Manual respectively. Title pages will be prepared in manuscript.

WAR DIARY
or
INTELLIGENCE SUMMARY.
(Erase heading not required.)

Army Form C. 2118.

Place	Date	Hour	Summary of Events and Information	Remarks and references to Appendices
FORCEVILLE	13/6/16		Company Training as usual. Rainy Weather.	
			Transport Lines still at HEDAUVILLE.	
"	14/6/16		Company Training as usual	
"	15/6/16		As for 14/6/16. Weather Fine. Nothing further to report.	
"	16/6/16		Company Training as usual.	
"	17/6/16		As for 16/6/16.	
"	18/6/16		Church Parade. Weather Fine.	
"	19/6/16		Company Training as usual.	
"	20/6/16		As for 19/6/16	
"	21/6/16		As for 19/6/16	
"	22/6/16		Company Training as usual. Weather Fine. [illegible] Orders to move [illegible]	
"	23/6/16		[illegible] [illegible]. Very heavy thunderstorm in the afternoon.	
		[illegible]	Left Forceville, [illegible] by transport, for Coisy via Canaples.	
Coisy	24/6/16	7am	Arrived Coisy. [illegible]	
"	25/6/16		Company Training as usual	
				G.O.P.

T2134. Wt. W708—776. 500000. 4/15. Sir J. C. & S.

WAR DIARY
or
~~INTELLIGENCE~~ SUMMARY.
(Erase heading not required.)

Instructions regarding War Diaries and Intelligence Summaries are contained in F. S. Regs., Part II. and the Staff Manual respectively. Title pages will be prepared in manuscript.

Army Form C. 2118.

Place	Date	Hour	Summary of Events and Information	Remarks and references to Appendices
CONTAY	25/6/16		Church Parade. Weather Fair.	
"	20/6/16		All surplus kit dumped at the 49th Divisional Dump.	
			Orders received to move to SENLIS VIA WARLOY at 12.10 am on the night of the 27/28th inst. Weather Fine. Nothing further to report.	
	28/6/16		Moved to SENLIS on the night of the 27/28th inst.	
SENLIS	1/7/16		Section moved to Assembly Trenches in AVELUY WOOD.	
			Transport Section at SENLIS.	
			Orders received to withdraw to VADENCOURT WOOD.	
VADENCOURT	4/7/16		Rest Billets in wood. Nothing to report.	
"	5/7/16		Moved from VADENCOURT & took over Assembly Trenches in AVELUY WOOD. Transport Lines between SENLIS & HEDAUVILLE.	

T2134. Wt. W708—776. 500000. 4/15. Sir J. C. & S.

147th Inf.Bde.
49th Div.

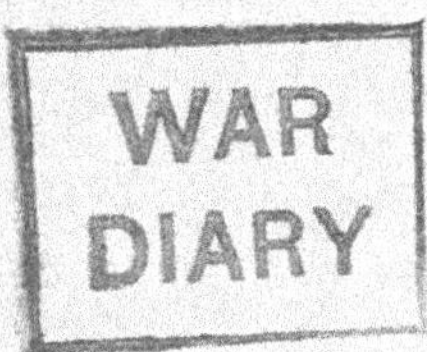

147th MACHINE GUN COMPANY.

J U L Y

1 9 1 6

Instructions regarding War Diaries and Intelligence Summaries are contained in F. S. Regs., Part II. and the Staff Manual respectively. Title pages will be prepared in manuscript.

WAR DIARY
or
INTELLIGENCE SUMMARY.
(*Erase heading not required.*)

147 M G Coy
Vol 7

Army Form C. 2118. 49

Place	Date	Hour	Summary of Events and Information	Remarks and references to Appendices
AVELUY WOOD.	1.7.16	12.30pm	Left AVELUY WOOD at 12.30 p.m. for CRUCIFIX DUGOUTS. Remained there for rest of day & night.	
CRUCIFIX DUGOUTS	2.7.16		In reserve at CRUCIFIX DUGOUTS	
		9 p.m.	Left dugouts at 9 p.m. & took over line between R.25.a.5.4. to R.25 c.4.4. No 4 Section with 4 guns in front line, No 3 Section at JOHNSTONE POST & remaining two sections at the bottom of PAISLEY AVENUE. Very heavy shelling during the whole evening & night. Casualties.	
THIEPVAL WOOD.	3.7.16.		Extended our line to the right to end of BISSET TRENCH & took over gun positions from 75th Bde. No 2 Section take over these positions. No 3 Sect. sent two guns to BISSET ST. No 1 Sect. take up positions along CAUSEWAY SIDE ST, CHATEAU ST. & ROSS ST. to ROSS CASTLE inclusive. Our dispositions then were. 10 guns in front line. 5 guns in second line. 1 gun in reserve. Heavy shelling throughout the day.	
do.	4.7.16.		The 77th Bde. took over some of our line on the right between BISSET ST & THIEPVAL AVENUE & thus relieved the two guns of No 3 Sect. which are then	

T2134. Wt. W708—776. 500000. 4/15. Sir J. C. & S.

GBJ

Instructions regarding War Diaries and Intelligence Summaries are contained in F. S. Regs., Part II. and the Staff Manual respectively. Title pages will be prepared in manuscript.

WAR DIARY
or
INTELLIGENCE SUMMARY.
(Erase heading not required.)

Army Form C. 2118.

Place	Date	Hour	Summary of Events and Information	Remarks and references to Appendices
THIEPVAL WOOD	4.7.16		placed in reserve. No 2 Sect. also withdrew two guns from front line.	
			Our dispositions then were.	
			6 guns in front line. 5 guns in second line. 5 guns in reserve.	
			Heavy shelling between 3 p.m. & 4.15 p.m.	
do.	5.7.16		Reconnoitred GEMMEL TRENCH & sited 4 M.G. emplacements as a second line defence. No 3 Section took up positions in this line.	
			Our dispositions then were.	
			6 guns in front line. 9 guns in second line. 1 gun in reserve.	
do.	6.7.16		Heavy shelling all day. No 2 Sect. relieved by No 3 Section.	
			One gun taken out of line near WHITCHURCH ST. & placed in reserve.	
do	7.7.16		Relieved by 148 Bde. M.G. Coy. No 2 Section being attached to them & remaining in GEMMEL ST. The remaining 3 sections proceeded to AVELUY WOOD ("A" TRENCHES). Relief complete. 5 A.M. 8.7.16.	
AVELUY WOOD	8.7.16		IN AVELUY WOOD Shelled during night.	
do.	9.7.16		Reserve in AVELUY WOOD. Relieved the 148 Bde. M.G. Coy. at 8 p.m. taking over line from THIEPVAL AVENUE to River ANCRE	

T2134. Wt. W708—776. 500000. 4/15. Sir J. C. & S.

Army Form C. 2118.

Instructions regarding War Diaries and Intelligence Summaries are contained in F. S. Regs., Part II. and the Staff Manual respectively. Title pages will be prepared in manuscript.

WAR DIARY
or
INTELLIGENCE SUMMARY.
(Erase heading not required.)

Place	Date	Hour	Summary of Events and Information	Remarks and references to Appendices
AVELUY WOOD.	9.7.16		Our dispositions then were.	
			4 guns in front line. 11 guns in second line. 1 gun in reserve.	
THIEPVAL WOOD	10.7.16.		Making emplacements along CHATEAU ST + ROSS ST.	
do	11.7.16.		Moved one gun from ROSS ST to emplacement near PETERHEAD SAP. to enfilade front S. Brigade on our left. Dispositions as for 9th inst	
do.	12.7.16.		As for 11th inst. Very Quiet Day.	
do.	13.7.16.		As for 11th inst.	
do.		3.45 am	Smoke barrage. M.G's fired indirect during barrage onto all German communication trenches leading to front line. Heavy fire brought to bear on FERME DE MOUQUET.	
do.	14.7.16		Moved reserve gun to house in HAMEL from which position, very good observation can be kept, on the enemy's line from R.24 a. 3.9. to R.24 a 10.9. This gun fired on any men seen in that area + worked in conjunction with an observer with telescope.	
do.	15.7.16		Quiet day dispositions as usual.	
	16.7.16		Fairly Quiet as for 15th inst.	
	17.7.16.		do.	

T2134. Wt. W708–776. 500000. 4/15. Sir J. C. & S.

Instructions regarding War Diaries and Intelligence Summaries are contained in F. S. Regs., Part II. and the Staff Manual respectively. Title pages will be prepared in manuscript.

WAR DIARY
or
INTELLIGENCE SUMMARY.
(Erase heading not required.)

Army Form C. 2118.

Place	Date	Hour	Summary of Events and Information	Remarks and references to Appendices
THIEPVAL WOOD.	18.7.16		As for 17.7.16.	
do.	19.7.16		do.	
do.	20.7.16		Fairly heavy shelling in morning.	
do	21.7.16		Fairly quiet day, disposition etc same.	
do.	22.7.16		Quiet do.	
do	23.7.16		do	
do	24.7.16		do.	
do.	25.7.16		Very heavy shelling from 12.30 to 5.15 p.m. Casualties 4 Killed 4 wounded	
do.	26.7.16		Quiet day dispositions etc as usual.	
do	27.7.16		do.	
do	28.7.16		Reconnoitred & commenced building two new emplacements at R.25.a.2.3 & Q.30 b.8.8.	
do	29.7.16		Quiet day disposition same.	
do	30.7.16		do do.	

T2134. Wt. W708—776. 500000. 4/15. Sir J. C. & S.

147th Brigade.

49th Division

147th BRIGADE MACHINE GUN COMPANY

AUGUST 1916

D.A.G.

3rd. Echelon.

Herewith WAR DIARY for 147 M.G.Coy

for the month of August 1916.

K J McIlwraith

147 Machine Gun Coy

Instructions regarding War Diaries and Intelligence Summaries are contained in F. S. Regs., Part II. and the Staff Manual respectively. Title pages will be prepared in manuscript.

WAR DIARY
or
INTELLIGENCE SUMMARY.
(Erase heading not required.)

Army Form C. 2118. 49

147 M G Coy 8

Vol 8

Place	Date	Hour	Summary of Events and Information	Remarks and references to Appendices
THIEPVAL WOOD.	1.8.16		Quiet day. Dispositions as usual.	
"	2.8.16		do. do	
"	3.8.16		do do	
"	4.8.16		do do	
"	5.8.16		do do	
"	6.8.16		do. do. Shelling shrapnel Cromarty Avenue	
		10.30pm. 11.30pm.	Casualties Two.	
"	7.8.16		Quiet day. Dispositions as usual. Nothing further to report.	
"	8.8.16		do do do.	
"	9.8.16		do for 8/8/16	
"	10.8.16		do	
"	11.8.16		do	
"	12.8.16		do	
"	13.8.16		do	
"	14.8.16		do.	

[illegible signature]

T2134. Wt. W708—776. 500000. 4/15. Sir J. C. & S.

Army Form C. 2118.

WAR DIARY
or
INTELLIGENCE SUMMARY.
(*Erase heading not required.*)

Instructions regarding War Diaries and Intelligence Summaries are contained in F. S. Regs., Part II. and the Staff Manual respectively. Title pages will be prepared in manuscript.

Place	Date	Hour	Summary of Events and Information	Remarks and references to Appendices
ARQUEVES.	25.8.16		Company Training. Manœuvres at CLAIRFAYE FARM. Practice "ATTACK" & CONSOLIDATION OF Captured Trenches.	
do	26.8.16		Company Training. Manœuvres at CLAIRFAYE FARM. Practice ATTACK & CONSOLIDATION OF Captured Trenches.	
do	27.8.16		Church Parade on ground east of RAINCHEVAL on RAINCHEVAL–ARQUEVES Road.	
		3.0pm	Left ARQUEVES suddenly for FORCEVILLE, VIA LEALVILLERS & ACHEUX.	
FORCEVILLE.		5.15pm	Arrived FORCEVILLE.	
do.	28.8.16		In rest billets.	
do	29.8.16	7.30am	Left FORCEVILLE for trenches Via HEDAUVILLE, BOUZINCOURT & MARTINSART WOOD. Relieved the 146th Machine Gun Company.	
THIEPVAL WOOD	29.8.16		All quiet.	
do.	30.8.16		All quiet.	
do.	31.8.16		Nothing to report. Dispositions as usual.	

T2134. Wt. W708–776. 500000. 4/15. Sir J. C. & S.

Army Form C. 2118.

Instructions regarding War Diaries and Intelligence Summaries are contained in F. S. Regs., Part II. and the Staff Manual respectively. Title pages will be prepared in manuscript.

WAR DIARY
or
INTELLIGENCE SUMMARY.
(Erase heading not required.)

Place	Date	Hour	Summary of Events and Information	Remarks and references to Appendices
THIEPVAL WOOD.	15.8.16.		Enemy registering on GEMMEL TRENCH with 5.9" shells. Gun position No 7 & gun etc blown in.	
do.	15-16 August		Indirect fire on Crucifix ~~about~~ in R.19a in conjunction with supposed GAS. offensive by 6th Division.	
	17.8.16		All quiet. Dispositions as usual.	
do	18.8.16.	5.2pm.	Smoke discharge. Fired indirect on THIEPVAL – GRANDCOURT Road.	
do	19.8.16		All quiet. Dispositions as usual.	
d	20.8.16		Infantry battalions of 147 Inf Bde relieved by 74 Inf Bde	
do	21.8.16		147 M. G. Coy relieved by 74 Machine Gun Coy. M.G. Coy proceed to ARQUEVES via MARTINSART, HEDAUVILLE, VARENNES, & LEALVILLERS.	
		6.30pm	Arrived ARQUEVES.	
ARQUEVES.	22.8.16		Re-fitting etc etc.	
do.	23.8.16		Company Training etc carried out.	
do	24.8.16		As for 23.8.16.	

T2134. Wt. W708—776. 500000. 4/15. Sir J. C. & S.

147th. INFANTRY BRIGADE

49th. DIVISION

147th. MACHINE GUN COMPANY

S E P T E M B E R 1 9 1 6.

D.A.G.
3rd Echelon

Herewith "WAR DIARY"
of 147 Machine Gun
Company. Sep 1916

[illegible] Capt
147 Machine Gun Coy.

Army Form C. 2118.

49

147 M G Coy

49

Vol 9

Instructions regarding War Diaries and Intelligence Summaries are contained in F. S. Regs., Part II. and the Staff Manual respectively. Title pages will be prepared in manuscript.

WAR DIARY
or
INTELLIGENCE SUMMARY.
(*Erase heading not required.*)

Place	Date	Hour	Summary of Events and Information	Remarks and references to Appendices
THIEPVAL WOOD	1.9.16.		Nothing to report.	
do.	2.9.16		Moved 6 guns up to tunnels etc prior to attack next morning. Two guns & one team lost through dug-out receiving two direct hits from MINENWERFER.	
do.	3.9.16.	5.10 am.	147 Infantry Brigade attacked German front line from R.19c.78.40. to R.19.c.4.6. & support line from R.19c. 88.53. to R.19c 3.8. The 146 Infantry Brigade attacking simultaneously on our left. Four of the guns were held up on East Hoyle trench owing to a small portion of the German line still holding out. The infantry were driven out & three of the machine guns mounting on parapet about the third parallel & getting good targets & covering retirement of our infantry. One gun lost subsequently recovered, two buried & one damaged by shrapnel. These guns were kept in position on 2nd & 3rd parallels & two more brought up to No 5 Tunnel in reserve. The 147 Inf Bde less M.G. Coy was relieved by 148 Inf Bde	

T2134. Wt. W708-776. 500000. 4/15. Sir J. C. & S.

Instructions regarding War Diaries and Intelligence Summaries are contained in F. S. Regs., Part II. and the Staff Manual respectively. Title pages will be prepared in manuscript.

WAR DIARY
or
~~INTELLIGENCE~~ SUMMARY.
(Erase heading not required.)

Army Form C. 2118.

Place	Date	Hour	Summary of Events and Information	Remarks and references to Appendices
THIEPVAL WOOD	4.9.16	10 am	Bombardment of enemy front line by our artillery, fairly heavy retaliation. Three Sections were relieved by 148. M. G. Coy. the remaining section being placed under orders of O.C. 148. M. G. Coy. Company moved to HEDAUVILLE to rest billets.	
HEDAUVILLE.	5.9.16		Company in Rest Billets.	
do	6.9.16		Training etc carried out.	
do	7.9.16		As for 6.9.16	
do	8.9.16		As for 6.9.16	
do	9.9.16		As for 6.9.16	
do.	10.9.16		Church Parade.	
do	11.9.16		Company training carried out.	
do	12.9.16		As for 11.9.16	
do	13.9.16		As for 11.9.16	
do	14.9.16		As for 11.9.16	
do.	15.9.16		As for 11.9.16	

RMS

T2134. Wt. W708—776. 500000. 4/15. Sir J. C. & S.

Instructions regarding War Diaries and Intelligence Summaries are contained in F. S. Regs., Part II. and the Staff Manual respectively. Title pages will be prepared in manuscript.

WAR DIARY
or
INTELLIGENCE SUMMARY.
(Erase heading not required.)

Army Form C. 2118.

Place	Date	Hour	Summary of Events and Information	Remarks and references to Appendices
HEDAUVILLE.	16.9.16.		Company moved to trenches occupied by the 147th Inf Bde & relieving the 32nd Machine Gun Coy in the line between THIEPVAL AVENUE & R32 c. 8.7. 4 Guns placed in front line, 2 in reserve in HINDENBURG TRENCH, 4 in AUTHUILLE	
AUTHUILLE WOOD.			DEFENCES, 2 in old BRITISH FRONT LINE, 4 in DUMBARTON CASTLE. Smoke barrage in afternoon in co-operation with an attack by the Canadians on the right. One Gun in front line & whole team knocked out by hostile artillery.	
AUTHUILLE WOOD.	17.9.16.		The 7th West Riding Regt. attacked & captured the German trenches from R31 a 9.1. to R31 c. 6.9. Machine Guns from DUMBARTON CASTLE & FIFTH AVENUE assisted by indirect firing into the trenches leading from THIEPVAL.	
	18.9.16.		Quiet day. Weather very wet. Nothing further to report.	

[signature]

Instructions regarding War Diaries and Intelligence Summaries are contained in F. S. Regs., Part II. and the Staff Manual respectively. Title pages will be prepared in manuscript.

WAR DIARY
or
INTELLIGENCE SUMMARY.
(Erase heading not required.)

Army Form C. 2118.

Place	Date	Hour	Summary of Events and Information	Remarks and references to Appendices
AUTHUILLE WOOD	19.9.16		Quiet morning. Artillery shelled LEIPZIG SALIENT during afternoon with 5.9's	
do.	20.9.16		Fairly quiet. Some shelling in LEIPZIG SALIENT.	
do	21.9.16		As for 20.9.16	
do.	22.9.16		As for. 20.9.16	
do	23.9.16		147 Inf. Bde relieved by 54th Infy. Bde. M.G. Coy remained in trenches under orders of G.O.C. 54 Inf. Bde. Fairly quiet day.	
do.	24.9.16		Company relieved by 54th Machine Gun Company in LEIPZIG SALIENT 2 Sections sent to 33rd M.G. Coy of the 11th Division 2 Sections & Headquarters in billets at AVELUY	
AVELUY & OVILLERS	25.9.16		2 Sections supported attack on right of THIEPVAL by 11th Division from SKYLINE TRENCH. Remaining two sections in reserve at AVELUY.	
do.	26.9.16		2 Sections in reserve at AVELUY 2 Sections attached to 11th Division	

[illegible signature]

T2134. Wt. W708—776. 500000. 4/15. Sir J. C. & S.

Instructions regarding War Diaries and Intelligence Summaries are contained in F. S. Regs., Part II. and the Staff Manual respectively. Title pages will be prepared in manuscript.

WAR DIARY
or
INTELLIGENCE SUMMARY.
(*Erase heading not required.*)

Army Form C. 2118.

Place	Date	Hour	Summary of Events and Information	Remarks and references to Appendices
AVELUY	27.9.16		Company in billets in AVELUY. Moved at night to huts in MAILLY WOOD.	
do.	28.9.16		Moved from MAILLY-MAILLET to GAUDIEMPE VIA BERTRANCOURT, COIGNEUX, SOUASTRE, ST AMAND.	
GAUDIEMPRE	29.9.16		147 Inf Bde relieved the 19th Inf Bde in the sector M. G. Coy in rest billets at GAUDIEMPRE.	
do.	30.9.16		Moved from rest billets in GAUDIEMPRE to the line relieving the 19th M.G. Coy in the sector HANNESCAMPS FONQUEVILLERS 5 guns in front line 2 guns at HANNESCAMPS 4 guns at FONQUEVILLERS round the defences 1 gun at CHISWICK AVENUE	

T2134. Wt. W708—776. 500000. 4/15. Sir J. C. & S.

147 Inf. Bde

~~Herewith~~ "WAR DIARY" of the 147th Machine Gun Company for the month of October 1916.

3.10.16

[signature] Major

147 Machine Gun Coy.

Instructions regarding War Diaries and Intelligence Summaries are contained in F. S. Regs., Part II. and the Staff Manual respectively. Title pages will be prepared in manuscript.

WAR DIARY
or
INTELLIGENCE SUMMARY.
(*Erase heading not required.*)

Army Form C. 2118.

147 M G Coy
Vol 10

Place	Date	Hour	Summary of Events and Information	Remarks and references to Appendices
BIENVILLERS	1.10.16		Very Quiet. Nothing to report. Weather Fine.	
do.	2.10.16		As for 1.10.16. Nothing further to report.	
do	3.10.16		147 Inf. Brigade. less 147 Machine Gun Company & 147 Trench Mortar Battery relieved by 148 Inf Brigade. 147 Machine Gun Company come under orders of G.O.C. 148 Inf. Brigade.	
do.	4.10.16		Bienvillers shelled by heavy hostile artillery.	
do.	5.10.16		All Quiet. Weather Raining all day.	
do	6.10.16		No 2 Section relieve No 1 Section in HANNESCAMPS. No 1 Section withdrawn to rest billets at HUMBERCAMPS. No 3 Section at FONQUEVILLERS relieved by a Section of the 146 Machine Gun Company & withdrawn to rest billets at HUMBERCAMPS. Two teams of No 4 Sections relieved by 146 Machine Gun Coy. These teams take up positions in HANNESCAMPS area. The positions of Guns. No 1. LAUSLEAGUE AVE. E.11.c.2.3. No 2 on ESSARTS Road. E17a 1.4. No 3. HANNESCAMPS. E.10.c.1.7. No 4 [illegible]	

T2134. Wt. W708—776. 500000. 4/15. Sir J. C. & S.

Instructions regarding War Diaries and Intelligence Summaries are contained in F. S. Regs., Part II. and the Staff Manual respectively. Title pages will be prepared in manuscript.

WAR DIARY
or
INTELLIGENCE SUMMARY.
(Erase heading not required.)

Army Form C. 2118.

Place	Date	Hour	Summary of Events and Information	Remarks and references to Appendices
BIENVILLERS	6.10.16		AVENUE E.16. 6.1.8. No 5. CONDUIT AVE E 16 c central. No 6. CHISWICK AVENUE E16 a. 6,5. No 7. E16 a. 95. 80 No 8. E16.c.4.5.	
do.	7.10.16		Fairly quiet. Weather Rainy.	
do.	8.10.16		Quiet. Weather Rainy Nothing further to report.	
do.	9.10.16		148 Inf Brigade relieved by 147 Inf Brigade.	
do.	10.10.16		BIENVILLERS Shelled by heavy hostile artillery. O.C. 147 Machine Gun Coy takes over command of 146 & 148 M. G. Coys whilst 147 Inf Bde occupies the line.	
do	11.10.16		BIENVILLERS Shelled during morning by heavy hostile artillery	
do.	12.10.16		No 1 Section relieve No 4 Section in the line HANNESCAMPS area. No 3 Section relieve No 2 Section in the line HANNESCAMPS area. Nos 2 & 4 Sections withdrawn to rest billets at HUMBERCAMPS	
do	13.10.16		Dispositions as usual. Fairly quiet. Nothing to report.	
	14.10.16		As for 13/10/16	
	15.10.16		As for 13/10/16	

[signature]

T2134. Wt. W708—776. 500000. 4/15. Sir J. C. & S.

Instructions regarding War Diaries and Intelligence Summaries are contained in F. S. Regs., Part II. and the Staff Manual respectively. Title pages will be prepared in manuscript.

WAR DIARY
or
INTELLIGENCE SUMMARY.
(Erase heading not required.)

Army Form C. 2118.

Place	Date	Hour	Summary of Events and Information	Remarks and references to Appendices
BIENVILLERS	16.10.16		Dispositions as usual. Quiet.	
do.	17.10.16		As for 16.10.16. Nothing to report.	
do.	18.10.16		147th Inf Bde relieved by 146 Inf Bde.	
			147 Machine Gun Company under orders of G.O.C. 146 Inf Bde	
do.	19.10.16		Whilst 146 Inf Bde 147 & 148 M.G. Coys come under the orders of O.C. 146 M.G. Coy.	
do.	20.10.16		No 4 Section relieve section 148 M.G. Coy	
			No 2 Section relieve Section 146 M.G. Coy.	
			No 3 Section relieve Section 146 M.G. Coy.	
			No 1 Section relieved by Section 146 M.G. Coy & withdrawn to rest billets at HUMBERCAMPS.	
			Disposition of Guns. 4 guns in front line 8 guns in FONQUEVILLERS defences 4 guns in reserve at HUMBERCAMPS.	
			Headquarters leave BIENVILLERS & are established at FONQUEVILLERS at E21, a. 9.5.10.	

[illegible signature]

T2134. Wt. W708—776. 500000. 4/15. Sir J. C. & S.

Army Form C. 2118.

Instructions regarding War Diaries and Intelligence Summaries are contained in F. S. Regs., Part II. and the Staff Manual respectively. Title pages will be prepared in manuscript.

WAR DIARY
or
INTELLIGENCE SUMMARY.
(Erase heading not required.)

Place	Date	Hour	Summary of Events and Information	Remarks and references to Appendices
FONQUEVILLERS	21.10.16		As for 20.10.16	
do	22.10.16		As for 20.10.16.	
do	23.10.16		No 1 Section leave HUMBERCAMPS & move to SOUASTRE Transport leave LA BAZEQUE FARM & move to SOUASTRE.	
do	24.10.16		All quiet Nothing to report	
do	25.10.16		As for 24.10.16.	
do	26.10.16		No 1 Section relieve No 3 Section in the line. No 3 Section move to rest billets in SOUASTRE.	
do	27.10.16		Dispositions as usual Nothing to report	
do	28.10.16		As for 27.10.16	
do	29.10.16		As for 27.10.16	
do	30.10.16		Heavy shelling in vicinity of MOUSE TRAP about K3 central	
do	31.10.16		Reserve gun at Headquarters mounted as aeroplane gun.	

[signature]

T2134. Wt. W708–776. 500000. 4/15. Sir J. C. & S.

Vol XI

WAR DIARY

of

147th M. G. Corps

November 1916.

Instructions regarding War Diaries and Intelligence Summaries are contained in F. S. Regs., Part II. and the Staff Manual respectively. Title pages will be prepared in manuscript.

WAR DIARY
or
INTELLIGENCE SUMMARY.
(Erase heading not required.)

Army Form C. 2118.

Place	Date	Hour	Summary of Events and Information	Remarks and references to Appendices
FONQUEVILLERS.	1.11.16		Hostile aeroplane driven away by M.G. fire at E.21.a.5.10.	
"	2.11.16		No3 Section relieved No1 Section. No1 Section relieved No4 Section in the FONQUEVILLERS defences. No4 Section to rest billets in SOUASTRE.	
			Area about N. End of FONQUEVILLERS heavily shelled during day with whezzbangs.	
"	3.11.16		Patrols out in direction of POPLARS. Fired during night on enemy parties working on wire near the 'Z'	
"	4.11.16		Fired during morning on enemy's wire & front line.	
"	5.11.16		Fired during early morning onto enemy's wiring parties. Night firing onto GOMMECOURT dump & tracks leading there.	
"	6.11.16		Same as for 05.11.16.	
"	7.11.16		Heavy M.G. fire directed during the night onto work at K.H.a. 9.8. which had been observed the previous day.	
"	8.11.16		Night firing from. E27b.5.1. & E27b.8.2. onto enemys tracks.	

A.B. Silliman Lt

T2134. Wt. W708—776. 500000. 4/15. Sir J. C. & S.

Instructions regarding War Diaries and Intelligence Summaries are contained in F. S. Regs., Part II. and the Staff Manual respectively. Title pages will be prepared in manuscript.

WAR DIARY
or
INTELLIGENCE SUMMARY.
(Erase heading not required.)

Army Form C. 2118.

Place	Date	Hour	Summary of Events and Information	Remarks and references to Appendices
FONQUEVILLERS.	9.11.16		Fired during night on working parties heard near the little 'Z'. Usual night firing onto tracks etc.	
do.	10.11.16		Same as for 9.11.16.	
do	11.11.16		As for 9.11.16.	
do.	12.11.16		No 2 Section relieve No 3 Section on Right. No 3 Section relieve No 1 Section on left. No 1 Section proceed to rest billets in SOUASTRE. No 4 Section remain in Centre positions.	
do.	13.11.16		Smoke barrage by Brigade. All guns firing during early morning from 5.45 am – 7.45 am on tracks & trenches etc in cooperation with attack on our right. about 27.000 rounds fired. Gun in BASTION moved to a position in front line on the LA BRAYELLE ROAD & manned by 146 M.G. Coy, part of BASTION filled in.	
do.	14.11.16		147 M.G. Coy now man gun in LA BRAYELLE RD. & gun at GENDARMERIE manned by 146 M.G. Coy.	

[signature illegible]

T2134. Wt. W708–776. 500000. 4/15. Sir J. C. & S.

Instructions regarding War Diaries and Intelligence Summaries are contained in F. S. Regs., Part II. and the Staff Manual respectively. Title pages will be prepared in manuscript.

WAR DIARY
or
INTELLIGENCE SUMMARY.
(Erase heading not required.)

Army Form C. 2118.

Place	Date	Hour	Summary of Events and Information	Remarks and references to Appendices
FONQUEVILLERS	15.11.16		GAS ALERT ordered. Kept gap in wire open during night at K4.a.2.7. by firing during night from "MOUSE TRAP".	
"	16.11.16		No 1 Section relieved No 2 Section on Right. No 2 Section relieve No 3 Section on Left. No 3 Section withdrawn to SOUASTRE No 4 Section remain in CENTRE. Bombardment of enemy's roads & tracks at 8 p.m & repeated at 9.15 p.m 10.30 p.m & 11 p.m. 3000 rounds fired at aeroplanes over FONQUEVILLERS. One driven away by our fire. Kept gap open at K4 a 2.7.	
"	17.11.16		Do for 16.11.16	
"	18.11.16		Steady fire maintained during night onto enemy's tracks etc & kept gap open at K.4 a 2.7.	
"	19.11.16		Two Lewis Gun teams attached to Coy for anti aircraft work from 1/5th Batt Lancashire Fusiliers. One in position at [illegible] the other at E27 a.7.2.	

[illegible signature]

T2134. Wt. W708—776. 500000. 4/15. Sir J. C. & S.

Army Form C. 2118.

WAR DIARY
or
INTELLIGENCE SUMMARY.
(Erase heading not required.)

Instructions regarding War Diaries and Intelligence Summaries are contained in F. S. Regs., Part II. and the Staff Manual respectively. Title pages will be prepared in manuscript.

Place	Date	Hour	Summary of Events and Information	Remarks and references to Appendices
FONQUEVILLERS	20.11.16		No 1 Section relieve No 2 Section on Left. No 2 Section relieve No 1 Section on Right. No 3 Section relieve No 4 Section in CENTRE. No 4 Section withdrawn to SOUASTRE. A successful raid carried out by 1/5. West Riding Regt the German trenches. A few Germans killed. No identification secured.	
"	21.11.16		Nothing to report	
"	22.11.16		As for 21.11.16.	
"	23.11.16		Heavy M.G. fire kept up on roads & tracks during the night.	
"	24.11.16		No 1 Section remain on left. No 2 Section withdrawn to SOUASTRE No 3 Section remain in CENTRE. No 4 Section relieve No 2 Section on Right. Fired 15.000 rds behind enemy's line during the night in retaliation to heavy M.G. fire on FONQUEVILLERS.	
"	25.11.16		As for. 24.11.16	
"	26.11.16		Fired 2000 rounds on enemy's wire from about K.3 central & kept up fairly heavy continuous fire from E27.b.8.2.	

A W Sellman [illegible]

T2134. Wt. W708—776. 500000. 4/15. Sir J. C. & S.

Instructions regarding War Diaries and Intelligence Summaries are contained in F. S. Regs., Part II. and the Staff Manual respectively. Title pages will be prepared in manuscript.

WAR DIARY
or
INTELLIGENCE SUMMARY.
(Erase heading not required.)

Army Form C. 2118.

Place	Date	Hour	Summary of Events and Information	Remarks and references to Appendices
FONQUEVILLERS	27.11.16		Enemy artillery quiet.	
"	28.11.16		No 1 Section withdrawn to SOUASTRE after relief by No 2 Section.	
"			Thorpe Street shelled during evening.	
"	29.11.16		SOUASTRE shelled by hostile artillery during the morning. Two shells landing in our horse lines. No damage done as horses had been withdrawn.	
"	30.11.16		Built new emplacement left of LINCOLN LANE. Old position temporarily abandoned owing to bad weather.	

[illegible signature]

T2134. Wt. W708—776. 500000. 4/15. Sir J. C. & S.

WO C12

CONFIDENTIAL

WAR DIARY

OF

147 Machine Gun Coy.

FROM 1-12-16 TO 31-12-16.

W M [illegible] Major

147 Machine Gun Coy.

Instructions regarding War Diaries and Intelligence Summaries are contained in F. S. Regs., Part II. and the Staff Manual respectively. Title pages will be prepared in manuscript.

WAR DIARY
or
INTELLIGENCE SUMMARY.
(Erase heading not required.)

Army Form C. 2118.

147 Machine Gun Coy

Place	Date	Hour	Summary of Events and Information	Remarks and references to Appendices
FONQUEVILLERS.	1.12.16		South end of FONQUEVILLERS shelled intermittently during the day. Very foggy. BJMS.	
"	2.12.16		Reliefs. No 1 Section relieved No 3 Section in the centre sector. No 3 Section to rest billets in SOUASTRE. FONQUEVILLERS shelled occasionally during the day with whizz bangs otherwise all quiet. BJMS.	
"	3.12.16		Hostile aeroplane activity about midday. Our anti-aircraft machine guns fired about 2000 rounds.	
	4.12.16		Quiet. Nothing further to report. BJMS	
"	5.12.16		147 M. G. Coy relieved in line by the 139 M. G. Coy. On relief whole Coy proceeded to rest billets in HALLOY via SOUASTRE, HENU, PAS, FAMECHON & HURTEBISE FARM. BJMS	
"	6.12.16		Coy moved from HALLOY to billets in CAUSMESNIL. BJMS	
"	7.12.16		Coy in billets at CAUSMESNIL. BJMS Company training carried on.	
"	8.12.16		Company training. Nothing further to report.	

[signature] Major
147 Machine Gun Coy.

T2134. Wt. W708—776. 500000. 4/15. Sir J. C. & S.

Instructions regarding War Diaries and Intelligence Summaries are contained in F. S. Regs., Part II. and the Staff Manual respectively. Title pages will be prepared in manuscript.

WAR DIARY
or
INTELLIGENCE SUMMARY.
(Erase heading not required.)

Army Form C. 2118.

Place	Date	Hour	Summary of Events and Information	Remarks and references to Appendices
CAUSMESNIL	9.12.16		Company Training carried out. Nothing further to report. WMS	
"	10.12.16		As for 9.12.16 WMS	
"	11.12.16		As for 10.12.16 WMS	
"	12.12.16		Inspection of 147 M. G. Coy by Lt. Col. Anderson, Corps Machine Gun Officer VII Corps. Weather very wet.	
"	13.12.16		Company Training carried out. WMS	
"	14.12.16		As for 13.12.16 WMS	
"	15.12.16		As for 14.12.16 WMS	
"	16.12.16		Company Training as usual. Nothing further to report. WMS	
"	17.12.16		As for 16.12.16 WMS	
"	18.12.16		As for 17.12.16 WMS	
"	20.12.16		Company Training. WMS	
"	21.12.16		As for 20.12.16 WMS	
"	22.12.16		As for 21.12.16 WMS	
"	23.12.16		Company Training carried out. Nothing further to report. WMS	
"	24.12.16		Sunday. Church Parade.	

WMS [illegible] Major
O.C. 147 Machine Gun Coy.

T2134. Wt. W708—776. 500000. 4/15. Sir J. C. & S.

Instructions regarding War Diaries and Intelligence Summaries are contained in F. S. Regs., Part II. and the Staff Manual respectively. Title pages will be prepared in manuscript.

WAR DIARY
or
INTELLIGENCE SUMMARY.
(Erase heading not required.)

Army Form C. 2118.

Place	Date	Hour	Summary of Events and Information	Remarks and references to Appendices
CAUSMESNIL	25.12.16		Xmas Day.	
"	26.12.16		Company Training carried on	
"	27.12.16		As for 26.12.16	
"	28.12.16		As for 27.12.16	
"	29.12.16		Inspection of Coy by Lt. Col Anderson Corps Machine Gun Officer [illegible] Corps. Practice Inspection & Column of Route formation. Weather Rainy	
"	30.12.16		Company Training as usual Nothing further to report.	
"	31.12.16		As for 30.12.16	

[illegible signature]
147 Machine Gun Coy.

T2134. Wt. W708—776. 500000. 4/15. Sir J. C. & S.

Vol 13

CONFIDENTIAL

WAR DIARY.

147 MACHINE GUN COY.

FROM 1. 1. 17.
TO. 31. 1. 17.

VOLUME.

[illegible signature]

Instructions regarding War Diaries and Intelligence Summaries are contained in F. S. Regs., Part II. and the Staff Manual respectively. Title pages will be prepared in manuscript.

WAR DIARY
or
INTELLIGENCE SUMMARY.
(Erase heading not required.)

Army Form C. 2118.

Place	Date	Hour	Summary of Events and Information	Remarks and references to Appendices
			147 Machine Gun Company.	
CAUSMESNIL	1.1.17		Company Training	WJMcS
	2.1.17		— do —	WJMcS
	3.1.17		— do —	WJMcS
	4.1.17		— do —	WJMcS
	5.1.17		— do —	WJMcS
	7.1.17		Nos 2, 4 & Hdqrs leave CAUSMESNIL for BERLES AU BOIS via HALLOY, HURTEBISE FARM, FAMECHON, PAS, GAUDEMPRE, HUMBERCAMPS, POMMIER. Nos 1 & 3 Sections leave HUMBERCAMPS for BERLES AU BOIS — No 1 Section taking up position in the B1 Sub Sector & No 3 Section in the Divisional Line	WJMcS
BERLES-AU-BOIS	8.1.17		No 2 Section take up positions in the B2 Sub Sector, and No 4 Section in reserve in BERLES. — 1 gun destroyed by shell fire on Divisional Line.	WJMcS
	9.1.17		Quiet day Nothing to report.	WJMcS
	10.1.17		— do — do —	WJMcS
	11.1.17		No 4 Section relieved No 1 Section in the B1 Sub Sector — No 1 Section proceeded to billets in HUMBERCAMPS. — No 3 Section relieved No 2 Section in the B2 Sub Sector — No 2 Section occupying emplacements in the Divisional Line.	WJMcS

W J McS [signature] Major
[illegible]

Instructions regarding War Diaries and Intelligence Summaries are contained in F. S. Regs., Part II. and the Staff Manual respectively. Title pages will be prepared in manuscript.

WAR DIARY
or
INTELLIGENCE SUMMARY.
(*Erase heading not required.*)

Army Form C. 2118.

147 Machine Gun Company

Place	Date	Hour	Summary of Events and Information	Remarks and references to Appendices
Berles au Bois	11.1.17	Centre	Sub Sector – No 2 Section occupying emplacements on the Divisional Line	[illegible]
	12.1.17		4 Machine Guns in W 17 d & W 18 c cooperated in an Artillery Strafe on Enemy front & support line about RANSART. During the evening 2 guns fired intermittently on to the S.E approaches about RANSART.	[illegible]
	13.1.17		Bombardment by heavies & field guns South of the B1 Sub Sector	[illegible]
	14.1.17		Nothing to report	[illegible]
	15.1.17		About 1000 rounds fired during the night from Ravine onto the S.E exits of RANSART.	[illegible]
	16.1.17		No 2 Section relieved No 3 Section in the B2 Sub Sector. No 3 Section occupying the Divisional Line – Nothing further to report.	[illegible]
	17.1.17		Nothing to report	[illegible]
	18.1.17		Nothing to report	[illegible]
	19.1.17		No 4 Section relieve No 1 Section in the B1 Sub Sector – No 1 Section proceeding to billets in HUMBERCAMPS – Work commenced on new emplacement at No 23. d. 17	[illegible]

[illegible signature]

T2134. Wt. W708–776. 500000. 4/15. Sir J. C. & S.

Instructions regarding War Diaries and Intelligence Summaries are contained in F. S. Regs., Part II. and the Staff Manual respectively. Title pages will be prepared in manuscript.

WAR DIARY
or
INTELLIGENCE SUMMARY.
(Erase heading not required.)

Army Form C. 2118.

Place	Date	Hour	Summary of Events and Information	Remarks and references to Appendices
			147 Machine Gun Company.	
BERLES AU BOIS	20.1.17		No 3 Section relieve No 2 Section in the R 2 Sub Sector. No 2 Section occupying emplacements on the Divisional Line.	KJMcL
	21.1.17		Our Artillery very active during the morning. Machine Gun fire as usual down the Ravine about W.17 d. We fired in to S.E approaches of RANSART during the night.	KJMcL
	22.1.17		Quiet day. Work commenced on restoring M.G. emplacement about W.23.c.45.30. Occasional bursts fired into RANSART during the night. I have found it absolutely essential to fire bursts at intervals during very cold weather.	KJMcL
	23.1.17		Following relief took place — No 1 Section relieved No 4 Section in R 1 Sub Sector, No 4 Section then occupying the Divisional Line. No 2 Section relieved No 3 Section in the R 2 Sub Sector, No 3 Section going out to rest billets in HUMBERCAMPS.	KJMcL
	24.1.17		The gun at W.24.a.5.6 was moved to a new position at junction of trench 106/107 (W.23.d.1.7.) An Anti aircraft gun was fitted up at Headquarters W.15.d.2.2.	KJMcL

K J McLaughlin
47 Machine Gun Coy

T2134. Wt. W708—776. 500000. 4/15. Sir J. C. & S.

Instructions regarding War Diaries and Intelligence Summaries are contained in F. S. Regs., Part II. and the Staff Manual respectively. Title pages will be prepared in manuscript.

WAR DIARY
or
INTELLIGENCE SUMMARY.
(Erase heading not required.)

Army Form C. 2118.

4?7 Machine Gun Coy.

Place	Date	Hour	Summary of Events and Information	Remarks and references to Appendices
BERLES-AU-BOIS.	25.1.17		Frost very keen during the night, trouble was experienced with the oil freezing, and it was found essential to keep firing bursts throughout the night.	WJMcS
	26.1.17		Nothing to report. Trouble still bang experienced with the oil	WJMcS
	27.1.17		No 4 Section relieved No 1 Section in the B1 Sub Sector. No 1 Section occupied on relief positions in the Divisional Line.	WJMcS
			No 3 Section relieved No 2 Section in the B2. Sub Sector. No 2 Section proceeded to rest billets in HUMBERCAMPS on relief.	
	28.1.17		During the night bursts were fired into RANSART, and enemy front line in front of RANSART.	WJMcS
	29.1.17		Artillery & trench mortars demonstration in afternoon. Nothing further to report.	WJMcS
	30.1.17		Details arranged for relief of 47 M. G. Coy in B. Sector by 137 M. G. Coy. Fire maintained in breaches in enemy's wire made by trench mortars previous day	WJMcS
	31.1.17		Berles shelled	WJMcS

W. J. Mc[illegible]

T2134. Wt. W708—776. 500000. 4/15. Sir J. C. & S.

Coron	Workmen's dwellings.
Cour des/aux marchandises	Goods yard.
Couvent	Convent.
Crassier	Slag heap.
Croix	Cross.
Darse	Inner dock.
Démoli - e	Destroyed.
Détruit - e, Dét^{t-e}	„
Déversoir	Weir.
Digue	Dyke, causeway.
Distillerie, Dist^{ie}	Distillery.
Douane / Bureau de douane	Custom-house.
Entrepôt de douane	Custom warehouse.
Dynamitière, Dynam^{re}	Dynamite magazine.
Dynamiterie	Dynamite factory.
Ecluse	Sluice, Lock.
Eclusette, Ecl^{te}	Sluice.
Ecole	School.
Ecurie	Stable.
Eglise	Church.
Emaillerie	Enamel works.
Embarcadère, Emb^{re}	Landing-place.
Estaminet, Estam^{t}	Inn.
Etang	Pond.
Fabrique, Fab^{e}	Factory.
Fab^{e} de produits chimiques	Chemical works.
Fab^{e} de faïence / Faïencerie	Pottery.
Ferme, F^{me}	Farm.
Filature, Fil^{re}	Spinning mill.
Fonderie, Fond^{ie}	Foundry.
Fontaine, Font^{ne}	Spring, fountain.
Forêt	Forest
Forme de radoub	Dry dock.
Forge	Smithy.
Fosse	Mine, Pit.
Fossé	Moat, Ditch.
Four	Kiln.
„ à chaux	Lime-kiln.

Four à coke	Coke oven.
Ganterie	Glove Factory.
Gare	Station.
Garenne	Warren.
Garnison	Garrison.
Gazomètre	Gasometer.
Glacerie / Fab^{e} de glaces	Mirror Factory.
Glacière	Ice factory.
Grue	Crane.
Gué	Ford.
Guérite	Sentry-box, Turret.
„ à signaux	Signal-box (Ry.)
Halte	Halt.
Hangar	Shed, Hangar.
Hôpital	Hospital.
Hôtel-de-Ville	Town hall.
Houillère	Colliery.
Huilerie	Oil factory.
Imprimerie, Impr^{ie}	Printing works.
Jetée	Pier.
Laminerie	Rolling mills.
Ligne / Laisse de haute marée	High water mark.
„ de basse marée	Low „ „
Maison Forestière / M^{on}. F^{re}.	Forester's house.
Malterie	Malt-house.
Marbrerie	Marble works.
Marais	Marsh.
Marais salant	Saltern, Salt marsh.
Marché	Market.
Mare	Pool.
Meule	Rick.
Minière	Mine.
Monastère	Monastery.
Moulin, M^{in}	Mill.
„ à vapeur	Steam mill.
Mur	Wall.
„ crénelé	Loop-holed wall.

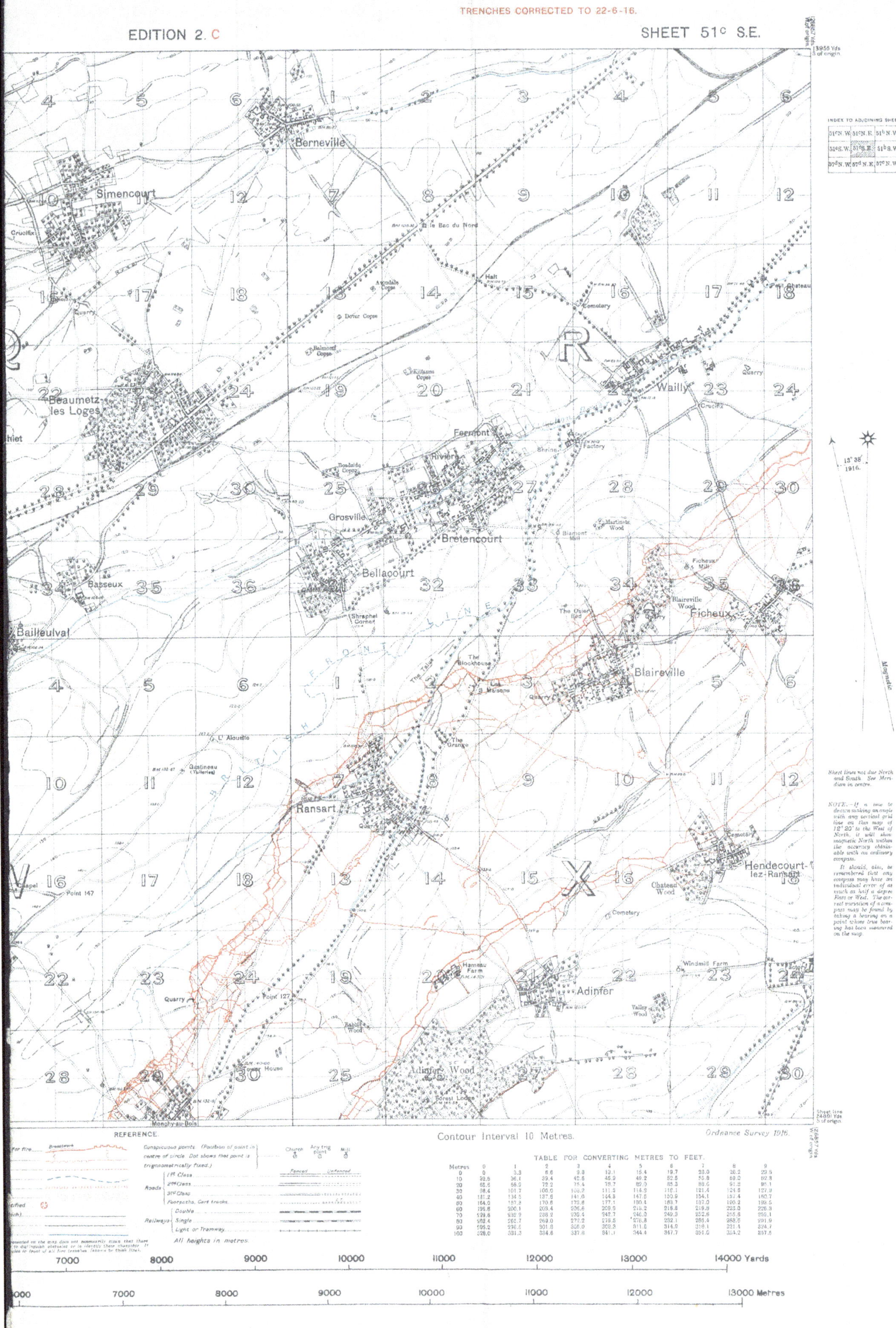

TABLE FOR CONVERTING METRES TO FEET.

Metres	0	1	2	3	4	5	6	7	8	9
0	0	3.3	6.6	9.8	13.1	16.4	19.7	23.0	26.2	29.5
10	32.8	36.1	39.4	42.6	45.9	49.2	52.5	55.8	59.0	62.3
20	65.6	68.9	72.2	75.4	78.7	82.0	85.3	88.6	91.9	95.1
30	98.4	101.7	105.0	108.2	111.5	114.8	118.1	121.4	124.6	127.9
40	131.2	134.5	137.8	141.0	144.3	147.6	150.9	154.1	157.4	160.7
50	164.0	167.3	170.6	173.8	177.1	180.4	183.7	187.0	190.2	193.5
60	196.8	200.1	203.4	206.6	209.9	213.2	216.5	219.8	223.0	226.3
70	229.6	232.9	236.2	239.4	242.7	246.0	249.3	252.6	255.8	259.1
80	262.4	265.7	269.0	272.2	275.5	278.8	282.1	285.4	288.6	291.9
90	295.2	298.5	301.8	305.0	308.3	311.6	314.9	318.1	321.4	324.7
100	328.0	331.3	334.6	337.8	341.1	344.4	347.7	351.0	354.2	357.5

GLOSSARY.

Abbaye, Abb^{e}	Abbey.
Abreuvoir, Ab^{r}	Watering-place.
Abri de douaniers	Customs-shelter.
Aciérie	Steel works.
Aiguilles	Points (Ry.)
Allée	Alley, Narrow road
Ancien - ne, Anc^{n-e}	Old.
Aqueduc	Aqueduct.
Arbre	Tree.
„ éventail	„ fan-shaped.
„ décharné	„ bare.
„ fourchu	„ forked.
„ isolé	„ isolated.
„ penché	„ leaning.
Arbrisseau	Small tree.
Arc	Arch.
Ardoisière, Ard^{re}	Slate quarry.
Arrêt	Halt.
Asile	Asylum.
„ des / d' aliénés	Lunatic asylum.
„ de charité / „ des pauvres / „ de refuge	Asylum.
Auberge, Aub^{ge}	Inn.
Aune	Alder-tree.
Bac	Ferry.
„ à traille	„
Bains	Baths.
Place aux bains	Bathing place.
Balise	Boom, Beacon.
Banc de sable	Sand-bank.
„ „ vase	Mud-bank.
Baraque	Hut.
Barrage	Dam.
Barrière	Gate, Stile.
(Machine à) Bascule	Weigh-bridge.
Bassin	Dock, Pond.
„ d'échouage	Tidal dock
Bassin de radoub	Dry dock.
Bateau phare	Light-ship.
Blanchisserie	Laundry.
B.M. (borne milliare)	Mile stone.
B^{e} (borne kilométrique)	
Boulonnerie / Fab^{e} de boulons	Bolt Factory.
Bouée	Buoy.
Brasserie, Brass^{ie}	Brewery.
Briqueterie, Briq^{ie}	Brickfield.
Brise-lames	Breakwater.
Bureau de poste	Post office.
„ de douane	Custom house.
Butte	Butt, Mound.
Cabane	Hut.
Cabaret, Cab^{t}	Inn.
Câble sous-marin	Submarine cable.
Calvaire, Calv^{e}	Calvary.
Canal de dessèchement	Drainage canal.
Canal d'irrigation	Irrigation canal.
Fab^{e} de caoutchouc	Rubber factory.
Carrière, Carr^{e}	Quarry.
„ de gravier	Gravel-pit.
Caserne	Barracks.
Champ de courses	Race course.
„ „ manoeuvres	Drill-ground.
„ „ tir	Rifle range.
Chantier	Building yard. / Ship yard. / Dock yard.
Chantier de construction	Slip-way.
Chapelle, Ch^{lle}	Chapel.
Charbonnage	Colliery.
Château d'eau	Water tower.
Chaussée	Causeway. / Highway.
Chemin de fer	Railway.
Cheminée, Ch^{née}	Chimney.
Chêne	Oak tree
Cimetière, Cim^{re}	Cemetery.
Clocher	Belfry.
Clouterie	Nail factory.
Colombier	Dove-cot.
Coron	Workmen's dwellings.
Cour des / aux marchandises	Goods yard.
Couvent	Convent.
Crassier	Slag heap.
Croix	Cross.
Darse	Inner dock.
Démoli - e	Destroyed.
Détruit - e, Dét^{t-e}	„
Déversoir	Weir.
Digue	Dyke, causeway.
Distillerie, Dist^{ie}	Distillery.
Douane / Bureau de douane	Custom-house.
Entrepôt de douane	Custom warehouse.
Dynamitière, Dynam^{re}	Dynamite magazine.
Dynamiterie	Dynamite factory.
Ecluse	Sluice, Lock.
Eclusette, Ecl^{te}	Sluice.
Ecole	School.
Ecurie	Stable.
Eglise	Church.
Emaillerie	Enamel works.
Embarcadère, Emb^{re}	Landing-place.
Estaminet, Estam^{t}	Inn.
Etang	Pond.
Fabrique, Fab^{e}	Factory.
Fab^{e} de produits chimiques	Chemical works.
Fab^{e} de faïence / Faïencerie	Pottery.
Ferme, F^{me}	Farm.
Filature, Fil^{re}	Spinning mill.
Fonderie, Fond^{ie}	Foundry.
Fontaine, Font^{ne}	Spring, fountain.
Forêt	Forest
Forme de radoub	Dry dock.
Forge	Smithy.
Fosse	Mine, Pit.
Fossé	Moat, Ditch.
Four	Kiln.
„ à chaux	Lime-kiln.
Four à coke	Coke oven.
Ganterie	Glove Factory.
Gare	Station.
Garenne	Warren.
Garnison	Garrison.
Gazomètre	Gasometer.
Glacerie / Fab^{e} de glaces	Mirror Factory.
Glacière	Ice factory.
Grue	Crane.
Gué	Ford.
Guérite	Sentry-box, Turret.
„ à signaux	Signal-box (Ry.)
Halte	Halt.
Hangar	Shed, Hangar.
Hôpital	Hospital.
Hôtel-de-Ville	Town hall.
Houillère	Colliery.
Huilerie	Oil factory.
Imprimerie, Impr^{ie}	Printing works.
Jetée	Pier.
Laminerie	Rolling mills.
Ligne / Laisse de haute marée	High water mark.
„ de basse marée	Low „ „
Maison Forestière / M^{on} F^{re}	Forester's house.
Malterie	Malt-house.
Marbrerie	Marble works.
Marais	Marsh.
Marais salant	Saltern, Salt marsh.
Marché	Market.
Mare	Pool.
Meule	Rick.
Minière	Mine.
Monastère	Monastery.
Moulin, M^{in}	Mill.
„ à vapeur	Steam mill.
Mur	Wall.
„ crénelé	Loop-holed wall.

Vol 14

Confidential.

War Diary

147 Machine Gun Coy

From 1. 2. 17 to 28. 2. 17.

Volume.

[signature] Major
147 Machine Gun Coy.

Instructions regarding War Diaries and Intelligence Summaries are contained in F. S. Regs., Part II. and the Staff Manual respectively. Title pages will be prepared in manuscript.

WAR DIARY
or
~~INTELLIGENCE SUMMARY.~~
(Erase heading not required.)

Army Form C. 2118.

Place	Date	Hour	Summary of Events and Information	Remarks and references to Appendices
			147 Machine Gun Coy.	
Bellacourt.	1.2.17		Relieved by 137 M.G. Coy, moved from Berles to billets in BELLACOURT via HUMBERCAMP. Transport at HUMBERCAMP.	
RIVIERE.	2.2.17		Company relieved 41st M.G. Coy in line in WAILLY trenches (F. Sector) Nos 1 & 2 Sections in left & right forward positions respectively Nos 4 & 3 Sections, left & right reserve positions respectively Headquarters at LE FERMONT - Transport BAILLEUVAL Situation quiet - Frost very severe.	
"	3.2.17		Nothing to report. Frost still holds.	
"	4.2.17		ditto ditto	
"	5.2.17		ditto ditto	
"	6.2.17		No 3 Section relieved No 2 Section in right forward positions Situation quiet - Weather conditions unchanged.	
"	7.2.17		Situation quiet. Weather conditions unaltered.	
"	8.2.17		No 4 Section relieved No 1 Section in left forward positions (7th & 8th 24 men arrived to join M.G.C. - 6 each from 4, 5, 6, & 7th Battalions W. R. Rgt.	

[signature]
147 Machine Gun Coy.

T2134. Wt. W708—776. 500000. 4/15. Sir J. C. & S.

Instructions regarding War Diaries and Intelligence Summaries are contained in F. S. Regs., Part II. and the Staff Manual respectively. Title pages will be prepared in manuscript.

WAR DIARY
or
~~INTELLIGENCE SUMMARY~~.
(Erase heading not required.)

Army Form C. 2118.

Place	Date	Hour	Summary of Events and Information	Remarks and references to Appendices
			147. Machine Gun Coy	
RIVIERE.	9.2.17		Situation & weather conditions unaltered – Enemy artillery more active than usual during day. During night 9/10 enemy M.G. active. Eighteen men left the Coy to proceed to M.G.C. Base.	A.S.
"	10.2.17		No 2 Section relieved No 3 Section in right forward positions. Situation quiet, weather conditions unchanged.	A.S.
"	11.2.17		Nothing to report.	A.S.
"	12.2.17		Enemy artillery shelled our lines fairly heavily in morning between FOREST & FICHEUX – Thaw set in.	A.S.
"	13.2.17		M.G. 3 fired on (100 rounds) and dispersed a German working party of about 30 men, which had been observed in front of their wire N.B. evening of 12th	A.S.
"	14.2.17		No 1 Section relieved No 4 Section in left Reserve line. No 3 Section relieved No 2 Section in right front line.	A.S.
"	15.2.17		Corps M.G.O. visited Coy H.Q. & M.G. positions etc in Brigade Sector. Work began on covered emplacement R.23.a.00.45.	A.S.

T2134. Wt. W708–776. 500000. 4/15. Sir J. C. & S.

B McSpoulder [signature]
147 Machine Gun Coy.

Instructions regarding War Diaries and Intelligence Summaries are contained in F. S. Regs., Part II. and the Staff Manual respectively. Title pages will be prepared in manuscript.

WAR DIARY

or

~~INTELLIGENCE SUMMARY.~~

(Erase heading not required.)

Army Form C. 2118.

Place	Date	Hour	Summary of Events and Information	Remarks and references to Appendices
			147. Machine Gun Coy	
RIVIERE	16.2.17		Rapid thaw set in. First rain for six weeks or more Situation. quiet.	
			M.G. 1 & 2 fired 600 rounds at enemy front line from R.29.c.8.2 & R.28.d.2.0. — M.G. 3 fired 300 rounds at enemy front line from R.29.d.7.9. & R.29.c.8.2.	[illegible]
"	17.2.17		A successful raid was carried out on German line by 4th West Riding Regt. at 10 pm. One prisoner taken, several casualties inflicted on enemy, dugouts bombed etc. Our casualties very light – 7 wounded.	
			147 M.G.C. assisted with 6 guns, rounds fired 9,250 rds.	
			No 3 section right gun in forward position fired 3,500 rds	[illegible]
"	18.2.17		No 2 section relieved No 3 section in "R" positions Situation quiet.	[illegible]
"	19.2.17		Situation quiet.	[illegible]
"	20.2.17		No 4 Section relieved No 1 Section in left positions	
			LE FERMONT shelled between 7.30 am & 9. am. Several enemy rifle grenades fell in front & reserve lines during day. Weather mild & rain.	

T2134. Wt. W708—776. 500000. 4/15. Sir J. C. & S.

[signature]
147 Machine Gun Coy

Army Form C. 2118.

Instructions regarding War Diaries and Intelligence Summaries are contained in F. S. Regs., Part II. and the Staff Manual respectively. Title pages will be prepared in manuscript.

WAR DIARY
or
~~INTELLIGENCE SUMMARY.~~
(Erase heading not required.)

Place	Date	Hour	Summary of Events and Information	Remarks and references to Appendices
			147 Machine Gun Coy	
RIVIERE.	21.2.17		M.G. 1 moved to new position. – Situation quiet. M.G. 2 moved to R.28.b.1.0. (firing right)	
〃	22.2.17		Situation quiet. No 3 Section relieved No 2 Section in right position.	
〃	23.2.17		Situation quiet M.G. at R4 fired 250 rounds on enemy trenches at M.31.a.	
	24.2.17		M.G. at R4 fired 250 rounds on tracks in enemy lines at M.31.a in retaliation for enemy M.G. fire. Situation quiet.	
	25.2.17		M.G. at R4 fired 600 rounds during night on (a) junction of roads R.36.a.6.5. (b) roads M31.b in retaliation for enemy M.G. fire.	
	26.2.17		No 1 Section relieved No 4 Section in left positions. No 2. Section relieved No 3. Section in right positions.	
	27.2.17		Five Officers & 25 O.R. attached from 44 M.G. Coy for instruction. Three Officers & 19 O.R^s in line, remainder at H.Q^rs. New covered M.G. emplacement R.23.d.00.45 completed	

[illegible signature]
147 Machine Gun Coy

Instructions regarding War Diaries and Intelligence Summaries are contained in F. S. Regs., Part II. and the Staff Manual respectively. Title pages will be prepared in manuscript.

WAR DIARY

~~or~~

~~INTELLIGENCE SUMMARY.~~

(Erase heading not required.)

Army Form C. 2118.

Place	Date	Hour	Summary of Events and Information	Remarks and references to Appendices
			144 Machine Gun Coy	
RIVIERE.	24.2.17		(Continued) N.B. Work of above, and any other description has been very difficult during the month, at first the very severe frost, then rapid thaw, causing the filling of sand bags to be very difficult, if not useless.	
	28.2.17		Situation quiet. Nothing to report.	

W. M. Spreadbury [illegible]
144 Machine Gun Coy.

T2134. Wt. W708—776. 500000. 4/15. Sir J. C. & S.

Vol 15

CONFIDENTIAL

WAR DIARY

of

147 Machine Gun
Company

From 1/3/17.

To 31/3/17.

[illegible] Major
147 [illegible]

Instructions regarding War Diaries and Intelligence Summaries are contained in F. S. Regs., Part II. and the Staff Manual respectively. Title pages will be prepared in manuscript.

WAR DIARY

or

~~INTELLIGENCE SUMMARY.~~

(Erase heading not required.)

Army Form C. 2118.

Place	Date	Hour	Summary of Events and Information	Remarks and references to Appendices
			147. Machine Gun Coy.	
RIVIERE	1.3.17		Company relieved in trenches by 44 M. G. Coy & proceeded to BAILLEUVAL where they remained for the night. AmS.	
BAILLEUVAL	2.3.17		Company left BAILLEUVAL 1 pm, arrived GRENAS 6 pm. AmS	
GRENAS	3.3.17		Day devoted to cleaning guns, men's equipment etc. AmS.	
	4.3.17		Church parade. AmS	
	5.3.17		Short route march by Sections & Section training. AmS.	
	6.3.17		Company left GRENAS 10.am arrived BOUQUEMAISON 1 pm. AmS.	
BOUQUEMAISON	7.3.17		Company left BOUQUEMAISON 2pm entrained at DOULLENS 2am (morning of the 8th). AmS.	
DOULLENS	8.3.17		Entrained DOULLENS 2.am, arrived MERVILLE 2pm – marched to VIEILLE CHAPELLE. AmS.	
VIEILLE CHAPELLE	9.3.17		Company relieved the 168 M. G. Coy in trenches FME DU BOIS Sector R.36.a.7.7. Transport – X11.b.2.2 H.Qrs Nos 1, 2 & 4 Sections in line. No 2. Section at H.Qrs. Brigade area RICHEBOURG S.W.3 1/10,000. – Northern boundary S.5.a.90.20 CHURCH ROAD (inclusive) and R NW (exclusive) S.22.c.45.00. S.27.a.60.85 S.26.b.80.85. continued O.L.	

T2134. Wt. W708–776. 500000. 4/15. Sir J. C. & S.

Instructions regarding War Diaries and Intelligence Summaries are contained in F. S. Regs., Part II. and the Staff Manual respectively. Title pages will be prepared in manuscript.

WAR DIARY
or
~~INTELLIGENCE SUMMARY.~~
(Erase heading not required.)

Army Form C. 2118.

147 Machine Gun Coy

Place	Date	Hour	Summary of Events and Information	Remarks and references to Appendices
			Continued:-	
RICHEBOURG	9.3.17		S.25. b. 90.35. One Section of 199 M.G. Coy in Sector with 3 M.G.s (under O.C. 147 M.G. Coy for discipline & tactics)	AMS
"	10.3.17		Situation quiet, nothing to report.	AMS.
"	11.3.17		ditto.	AMS
"	12.3.17		Transport lines shelled during morning. M.G. EDWARDS POST fired 250 rounds during night on Cross Roads S.14.a. in retaliation for enemy M.G. fire Aeroplane gun at EDWARDS POST fired 400 rounds at hostile aeroplanes. Hostile artillery active throughout day	AMS
"	13.3.17		M.G. at EDWARDS POST fired 500 rounds during night on DISTILLERY S.14 in retaliation for enemy M.G. fire. No 2 Section relieved No 3 Section in line. Night positions.	AMS
"	14.3.17		M.G. at EDWARDS POST fired 250 rounds (1) DISTILLERY S.14 (2) CROSS ROADS S.14.a. during night for the purpose of (1) Harrasing enemy dump (2) Retaliation for enemy M.G. fire.	AMS.
"	15.3.17		M.G. at EDWARDS POST fired 500 rounds on DISTILLERY S.14 during night in retaliation for enemy M.G. fire. Continued:	

[signature]

T2134. Wt. W708—776. 500000. 4/15. Sir J. C. & S.

Instructions regarding War Diaries and Intelligence Summaries are contained in F. S. Regs., Part II. and the Staff Manual respectively. Title pages will be prepared in manuscript.

WAR DIARY
or
~~INTELLIGENCE SUMMARY.~~
(Erase heading not required.)

Army Form C. 2118.

Place	Date	Hour	Summary of Events and Information	Remarks and references to Appendices
			Continued 147. Machine Gun Coy.	
RICHEBOURG	15.3.17		M. G. S.4.c.18.88 fired 2000 rounds during night (6 pm – 11.30 pm) on CROSS ROADS LA TOURELLE, elevating up to DISTILLERY S.14.a.84.40 retaliation on enemy M. G. fire. During the day 6" battery, 400 yds from H. Qrs Sloans Square, heavily shelled by 4.2 – 5.9 & 8". Amb.	
"	16.3.17		M. G. at EDWARDS POST fired 500 rounds on CROSS ROADS S.14.a. during night, retaliation for enemy M. G. fire. M. G at S.4.c.18.88 fired 750 rounds on crossing of NORTH TRENCH S.14.c.00.53. in enemy lines – 10 pm – 1 am. Amb.	
"	17.3.17		No 3 Section relieved No 4 Section in line (Right Centre positions) M. G. at M.34.c.7.5 fired 750 on S14 central 6.30pm – 10pm in retaliation for enemy M. G. fire. Work on dugout at HILL REDOUBT begun by 168 M. G. Coy completed this day by No1. Section Amb.	
"	18.3.17		M. G. at EDWARDS POST fired 500 rounds on DISTILLERY 6.30 pm to 3. am. M. G. at M.34.c.7.5 fired 750 rounds on S.14 central 6.30 pm to 10 pm. Amb.	
"	19.3.17		M. G. at EDWARDS POST fired 500 rounds on ROAD JUNCTIONS Contd.	

[signature]

T2134. Wt. W708—776. 500000. 4/15. Sir J. C. & S.

Instructions regarding War Diaries and Intelligence Summaries are contained in F. S. Regs., Part II. and the Staff Manual respectively. Title pages will be prepared in manuscript.

WAR DIARY
or
~~INTELLIGENCE SUMMARY.~~
(Erase heading not required.)

Army Form C. 2118.

Place	Date	Hour	Summary of Events and Information	Remarks and references to Appendices
			147 Machine Gun Coy.	
			Cont'd.	
RICHEBOURG	19.3.17		S12.c.6.5 6pm–12pm. M.G. at S4.c.18.88 fired 750 rounds on S.17.a.87.40 7.15pm–8.15pm & 10pm to 11.30pm.	AmB.
"	20.3.17		M.G. EDWARDS POST fired 500 rounds S12.c.6.5. roads S.11.d.4.2	com trench 11pm 1pm AmB.
"	21.3.17		No 4 Section relieved No 1 Section in line – M.G. PONT LOGUE fired 1750 rounds at X roads S6.a.8.7. 7.30pm–10.30pm. PONT LOGIE fired 250 rounds at hostile aeroplane 4.45pm & drove same back. M.G. S.9.a.2.8 fired 500 rounds at hostile aeroplane and drove same back. S.9.b.2.7 fired 600 rounds at enemy C.T. S17.c.15.50. S11.d.3.2 & CROSS ROADS S12.c.55.50. 7pm & 10.15pm.	AmB.
"	22.3.17		M.G. at EDWARDS POST fired 1000 rounds at ROAD JUNCTION S12.c.6.5. 8.45pm–11.15pm. M.G. S.4.a.95.90. fired 1000 rounds LA BASSEE RD S11.c.5.3.–S17.a.8.6. & S6.a.61.87. 9pm–11.30pm. Three men of No 2 Section wounded by shrapnel, Pte Gunn, Pte Scarueside, & Womersley (the last two remained at duty)	AmB.

W. McSomerville Major

T2134. Wt. W708–776. 500000. 4/15. Sir J. C. & S.

Instructions regarding War Diaries and Intelligence Summaries are contained in F. S. Regs., Part II. and the Staff Manual respectively. Title pages will be prepared in manuscript.

WAR DIARY

or

~~INTELLIGENCE SUMMARY.~~

(Erase heading not required.)

Army Form C. 2118.

Place	Date	Hour	Summary of Events and Information	Remarks and references to Appendices
			147 Machine Gun Coy	
RICHEBOURG	23.3.17		M. G. at EDWARDS POST fired 250 rounds S14 c.2.5 to S14 c 4.0. 6.30 pm – 7 pm. M. G. at S4 a. 95.90 fired 1,000 rounds on (1) LA BASSEE RD (2) S. ~~6.c~~ 6.a. 61.84 8.30 – 12 pm.	AWS.
"	24.3.17		M. G. S.9.d 28 fired 500 rounds at enemy aeroplane flying over our lines at following times 9.30 am – 10.5 am & 10.30 am. Aeroplane disappeared at 10.30 am. EDWARDS POST fired 250 rounds on S. 14.c.3.4 to S. 23.a.9.8 7.30 pm to 8 pm. M. G S. 4.a 95.90 fired 550 rounds S11.c.5.3. – 17.a 8.6. & S6.a.61. – 87 7.15 pm 9.30 pm. Anti aircraft gun fired 350 rounds at hostile aeroplane at 2.15 pm & 4.30 pm	AWS.
"	25.3.17		No 1. Section relieved No 2 Section in line. Section of 199th M. G. C at LANSDOWNE POST withdrawn from 147th area. & the 2 positions held by them in "B" line taken over by teams of 147 M. G. C. M. G. at S4. a. 95.90 fired 500 rounds at BOIS DE BIEZ 8.30 pm – 11.30 pm.	AWS.
"	26.3.17		M. G at HILL REDOUBT taken over by the 148 M. G. C. M. G. S4. a. 95.90 fired 750 rounds on BOIS DU BIEZ 9 pm – 3. am	

[signature]

T2134. Wt. W708–776. 500000. 4/15. Sir J. C. & S.

Instructions regarding War Diaries and Intelligence Summaries are contained in F. S. Regs., Part II. and the Staff Manual respectively. Title pages will be prepared in manuscript.

WAR DIARY
or
INTELLIGENCE ~~SUMMARY~~.
(Erase heading not required.)

Army Form C. 2118.

Place	Date	Hour	Summary of Events and Information	Remarks and references to Appendices
			147. Machine Gun Coy	
RICHEBOURG.	27.3.17		M. G. EDWARDS POST fired 1,000 rounds on SERPENT TRENCH S22 b 9.30pm - 11pm	AmB
"	28.3.17		Two Portugese Officers & one Portugese N.C.O attached to Coy for instruction	AmB
"	29.3.17		A raid was carried out by 6th Bttn West Riding Regt on enemy trenches at S10. d. 58.62 In conjunction with the raid, the 147th M. G. Coy co-operated as follows:- EDWARDS POST. M. G. 2500 rounds south of SHEPHERDS REDOUBT & DISTILLERY. — TONY LOGY M.G. 4.000 rounds LA BASSEE RD from S11. C. 35. 75 to DISTILLERY & trench from S11. C. 25. 65 to S11. C. 5. 3. — M. G at S8. d. 85. 30 fired 1625 rounds on STEPHENS WALK from S11. C. 50. 25. to S11. d. 4. 1. — M. G. at S14. b 40. 05 fired 1650 rounds, enfilading MITZI trench. The above firing was "rapid" from ZERO (2 am) till ZERO & 30 minutes — No 4 Section had three casualties (2 killed & 1 wounded) caused by a shell bursting in a dug-out. M. G at S.4. a. 95. 90 fired 500 rounds on LA BASSEE RD 8 pm — 10.30 pm.	AmB.
"	30.3.17		No 2. Section relieved No 3 Section in line. Work (with sandbags etc) begun 19th March by No 3 Section at continued.	

T2134. Wt. W708—776. 500000. 4/15. Sir J. C. & S.

[illegible signature]

Army Form C. 2118.

Instructions regarding War Diaries and Intelligence Summaries are contained in F. S. Regs., Part II. and the Staff Manual respectively. Title Pages will be prepared in manuscript.

WAR DIARY
or
~~INTELLIGENCE SUMMARY~~
(Erase heading not required.)

Place	Date	Hour	Summary of Events and Information	Remarks and references to Appendices
			Continued 147. Machine Gun Coy	
RICHEBOURG.	30.3.17		Section H.Q. S.9.d.3.4 completed on 30th March by No 1 Section. M.G. at S.4.a.95.90 fired 500 rounds at LA BASSEE RD. 8pm – 10pm	[illegible]
	31.3.17		~~Nothing to report.~~ Headquarters moved to Transport lines at X.10.c.3.4 owing to heavy shelling	[illegible]

[illegible signature]

2449 Wt. W14957/M90 750,000 1/16 J.B.C. & A. Forms/C.2118/12.

Vol 16

* * C O N F I D E N T I A L * *

----

* W A R D I A R Y *

of the

147th MACHINE GUN COMPANY

From 1-4-17.

To 30-4-17.

Volume.

[signature] Major.

Commdg. 147th Machine Gun Company.

Instructions regarding War Diaries and Intelligence Summaries are contained in F. S. Regs., Part II. and the Staff Manual respectively. Title pages will be prepared in manuscript.

WAR DIARY
or
~~INTELLIGENCE SUMMARY.~~
(Erase heading not required.)

Army Form C. 2118.

Place	Date	Hour	Summary of Events and Information	Remarks and references to Appendices
			144 Machine Gun Coy.	
RICHEBOURG.	1.4.17		M. G. S.9.b.2.9 fired 750 rounds on NOTRA TRENCH and from S.4.a.9.0 to S.23.b.9.3 – 10.30pm – 11pm.	A.B.
	2.4.17		Heavy Snow storms – Transport inspected by Corps M.G. Officer M.G. S.4.a.75.90 fired 250 rounds on hostile aeroplane 9.15.am	A.B.
	3.4.17		Nothing to report.	A.B.
	4.4.17		M.G. at S.4.a.95.90 fired 750 rounds on LA BASSEE RD past DISTILLERY from 8.pm onwards in retaliation for enemy M.G. fire on PONT LOGY.	A.B.
	5.4.17		144 M.G. Coy relieved in FERME DU BOIS Sector by 199th M.G. Coy 144 M.G. Coy with Transport in billets VIEILLE CHAPELLE 36.a.S.E. R 29.c.9.8.	A.B.
VIEILLE CHAPELLE.	6.4.17		Day devoted to cleaning guns + equipment	A.B.
	7.4.17		Company training	A.B.
	8.4.17		Church Parade at VIEILLE CHAPELLE.	A.B.
	9.4.17		Company training.	A.B.
	10.4.17		Company training	A.B.

2353 Wt. W2544/1454 700,000 5/15 D. D. & L. A.D.S.S./Forms/C. 2118.

Army Form C. 2118.

WAR DIARY
or
~~INTELLIGENCE SUMMARY.~~
(Erase heading not required.)

Instructions regarding War Diaries and Intelligence Summaries are contained in F. S. Regs., Part II. and the Staff Manual respectively. Title pages will be prepared in manuscript.

Place	Date	Hour	Summary of Events and Information	Remarks and references to Appendices
			147 Machine Gun Coy	
VIEILLE CHAPELLE	11.4.17		Transport Section inspected by Col. Haigh. O.C. Divn Train	AnB
	12.4.17		Company training	AnB
	13.4.17		— ditto —	AnB
	14.4.17		— ditto —	AnB
	15.4.17		Church parade VIEILLE CHAPELLE.	AnB
	16.4.17		Company training	AnB
	17.4.17		— ditto —	AnB
	18.4.17		— ditto —	AnB
	19.4.17		— ditto —	AnB
RICHEBOURG	20.4.17		Company relieved the 199 M.G. Coy in line FERME DU BOIS Sector. No 1 Section in reserve - No 3 Section LEFT positions No 4 Section RIGHT positions, No 2 Section CENTRE positions Company Headquarters & Transport at X.10.c.4.4.	AnB
	21.4.17		M.G. at PONT LOGY fired 1,000 rounds during night on LA BASSEE RD at DISTILLERY.	AnB
	22.4.17		M.G. at EDWARDS POST fired 2000 rounds during night on QUINQUE RUE between S.22.b.40/95. & CROSS ROADS S.14.a.85.70.	AnB

2353 Wt. W2544/1454 700,000 5/15 D. D. & L. A.D.S.S./Forms/C. 2118.

Army Form C. 2118.

WAR DIARY
or
~~INTELLIGENCE SUMMARY.~~
(Erase heading not required.)

Instructions regarding War Diaries and Intelligence Summaries are contained in F. S. Regs., Part II. and the Staff Manual respectively. Title pages will be prepared in manuscript.

144 Machine Gun Coy.

Place	Date	Hour	Summary of Events and Information	Remarks and references to Appendices
RICHEBOURG	23.4.17		M. G at PONT LOGY fired 3,000 rounds on LA BASSEE RD and swing traverse to edge of BIEZ WOOD during night. M. G at EDWARDS POST fired 3000 rounds on DISTILLERY, S 17 Central & QUINQUE RUE S 17. d. 85. 17 C. 00 10 pm to 12 pm.	[initials]
	24.4.17		No 1. Section relieved No 2. Section in CENTRE positions M. G at S 4. d. 07. 02. ORCHARD left of LA BASSEE RD fired 3000 rounds on tracks and roads S. 6. d. 5. 7 and S 12. a. 3. 1, also swinging traverse between these points, during night. M. G at EDWARDS POST fired 3,000 rounds on DISTILLERY S 17 Central, and QUINQUE RUE. S 17. a. 85 – C. 06 – 9.15 pm to 12 Midnight.	[initials]
	25.4.17		M. G at EDWARDS POST fired 3,000 rounds on DISTILLERY QUINQUE RUE & NORA TRENCH 8. pm – 10.30 pm. M. G at S. 4. d. 07. 02 fired 3500 rounds on tracks at LA ROSSE dump and tramway at edge of RAYMOOD RD past DISTILLERY also traverse between these points – during night.	[initials]

2353 Wt. W2544/1454 700,000 5/15 D. D. & L. A.D.S.S./Forms/C. 2118.

Army Form C. 2118.

Instructions regarding War Diaries and Intelligence Summaries are contained in F. S. Regs., Part II. and the Staff Manual respectively. Title pages will be prepared in manuscript.

WAR DIARY
or
INTELLIGENCE SUMMARY.
(Erase heading not required.)

147 M.G. Coy

Place	Date	Hour	Summary of Events and Information	Remarks and references to Appendices
RICHEBOURG	26.4.17.		EDWARDS POST M.G. fired 3000 rounds on DISTILLERY, QUINQUE RUE & NORA TRENCH 11 pm – 1.30 am. S.4.d.07.02 ORCHARD left of LA BASSEE RD fired 3850 rounds, swinging traverse from S.d.5.8 (LA RUSSEE dump) to S.14.a.9.6 (LA TOURELLE) on points STEPHENS WALK, SUSANS TRENCH, LIGNY LE PETIT, and tramways behind BIEZ WOOD.	A.B.
	27.4.17		M.G. at EDWARDS POST fired 3.000 rounds on DISTILLERY, QUINQUE RUE & NORA TRENCH 2.am – 4.30 am. S.4.d.07.02 ORCHARD left of LA BASSEE RD fired 3100 rounds on LA BASSEE RD by DISTILLERY, LIGNY LE PETIT, LA RUSSE DUMP, tramway running from S.12.a.4.3 to S.12.d.3.7 during the night.	A.B.
	28.4.17		No 2 Section relieved No 3 Section in "LEFT" positions. M.G. at EDWARDS POST fired 2,000 rounds at LA TOURELLE, DISTILLERY, NORA TRENCH 8.15 – 10.30 pm. M.G. at M.34.d.2.1 fired 3140 rounds on tracks at S.6.d.7.5. FME DU BOIS S.12.c.15.25. TRENCH JUNCTION S.11.d.45.05. TRENCH from S.12.a.3.1 to C.5.9.	A.B.

2353 Wt. W2544/1454 700,000 5/15 D. D. & L. A.D.S.S./Forms/C. 2118.

Instructions regarding War Diaries and Intelligence Summaries are contained in F. S. Regs., Part II. and the Staff Manual respectively. Title pages will be prepared in manuscript.

WAR DIARY
or
~~INTELLIGENCE SUMMARY.~~
(Erase heading not required.)

Army Form C. 2118.

Place	Date	Hour	Summary of Events and Information	Remarks and references to Appendices
			47. Machine Gun Company.	
RICHEBOURG	29.1.17		M.G. at EDWARDS POST fired 2500 rounds on DISTILLERY, NORA TRENCH, QUINQUE RUE, LE TOURELLE to NORA TRENCH. 11.30 pm – 2 am. M.G. M.3 & d.21. fired 3320 rounds on TRAMWAY JUNCTION S12 b.5.7 TRENCH TRAMWAY ROAD JUNCTIONS S.12 c 30.65 to C.70.45, TRACK JUNCTION S.11.d 80.35 & S 6 a.90.35. Bursts fired at intervals throughout the night from 9 pm – 3.30 am.	A.B.
	30.1.17		Nothing to report	A.B.

2353 Wt. W2544/1454 700,000 5/15 D. D. & L. A.D.S.S./Forms/C. 2118.

Vol 17

Confidential.

War Diary

of

147th Machine Gun Coy.

From 1. 5. 17.

To 31. 5. 17.

[illegible] Major
[illegible] Machine Gun Coy

Instructions regarding War Diaries and Intelligence Summaries are contained in F. S. Regs., Part II. and the Staff Manual respectively. Title pages will be prepared in manuscript.

WAR DIARY
or
~~INTELLIGENCE SUMMARY.~~
(Erase heading not required.)

Army Form C. 2118.

Place	Date	Hour	Summary of Events and Information	Remarks and references to Appendices
			147 Machine Gun Company.	
RICHEBOURG	1.5.17		M.G. firing for last 48 hours. M.G. EDWARD'S POST fired 2.000 rounds on (1) DISTILLERY, (2) LE TOURELLE, (3) NORA TRENCH, (4) QUINQUE RUE, 2 am – 4 am. also fired 100 rounds at hostile plane. MG at 34 d. 2.1. fired 2.980 rounds on TRENCH JUNCTION S11d. 85.80, TRACK JUNCTION S6d. 90.35, TRAMWAY JUNCTION S12 b. 5.7 and ROAD S12.C.5.5 – d. 2.7, bursts at intervals 9 pm – 4 am. MG. EDWARD'S POST fired 1500 rounds on QUINQUE RUE and NORA TRENCH, 8.30 pm – 11 pm. A.A. Gun fired 1,000 rounds at hostile aeroplane, 7.35 am – 9.45 am at intervals. MG. M.34 d. 2.1 fired 3170 rounds on (1) TRENCH TRAMWAY S12 a. 6.2 to d. 3.7 (2) ROAD JUNCTION S12 C 15.05, (3) ROAD S17 b. 3.9 — 11 d. 8.3. (4) HOUSE AND TRACK S.6.d 7.6, bursts at intervals throughout the night from 9 pm – 3.45 am. AmB.	
	2.5.17		No. 3 Section relieved No. 4 Section in "right positions. MG. at EDWARD'S POST fired 3100 rounds on LA TOURELLE CROSS ROADS, S17c. 85.60, DISTILLERY S.17 central, NORA TRENCH S17 C.05 to S23a. 9.8, 9.30 pm – 2.30 am. MG M.34 d.2.1. fired 3250 rounds on TRACK JUNCTION S6.d. 90.35, ROAD S.12.C.15.05 – 18.a.30.85, TRENCH S11d. 7.5 — d.85.30, TRENCH JUNCTION S11d. 45.10. during night. AmB.	

Instructions regarding War Diaries and Intelligence Summaries are contained in F. S. Regs., Part II. and the Staff Manual respectively. Title pages will be prepared in manuscript.

WAR DIARY
or
~~INTELLIGENCE SUMMARY.~~
(Erase heading not required.)

Army Form C. 2118.

Place	Date	Hour	Summary of Events and Information	Remarks and references to Appendices
			144 Machine Gun Company	
RICHEBOURG	3.5.17		M.G. at EDWARD'S POST fired 2750 rounds on (1) LA TOURELLE CROSS ROADS, (2) NORA TRENCH, (3) LA TOURELLE FARM, 10.30 pm – 4 am. MG M34 a.2.1 fired 3.000 rounds on TRAMWAY JUNCTION S.12 b. 5.7, ROAD JUNCTION S11 d 80.25, TRENCH JUNCTION S11 d 45.10, ROAD S12 c 15.05 to 12 c 65.50 during night. Amb.	
	4.5.17		MG at EDWARD'S POST fired 3250 rounds on LA TOURELLE FARM and DISTILLERY 10 pm – 2 am. MG at M. 34 a.2.1. fired 3100 rounds on (1) ROAD S.12 c. 15.05, (2) ROAD S.12 c. 35.75, (3) TRENCH JUNCTION S11 d. 85.35 (4) ROAD JUNCTION S. 11 c 85.60, 9 pm to 4 am. Amb.	
	5.5.17		MG at EDWARD'S POST fired 2750 rounds on LA TOURELLE FARM, TRACK and CROSS ROADS, 9.30 pm – 12.30 am. MG at M34 d.2.1. fired 3350 rounds on (1) ROAD S12 c. 5.9 (2) FME DU BIEZ S.12 c 15.25, (3) HOUSE and TRAMWAY S12 b.25.90, (4) TRENCH JUNCTION S11 d. 45.10, 9 pm – 3.3 am. Work begun by No 3 Section on new "right" section HQ at 9.c.5.5 RICHEBOURG. Dug-out being constructed in house for Section; – two concrete emplacements already existing. Amb.	
	6.5.17		M.G at EDWARD'S POST fired 2000 rounds on usual targets during the night. MG at M.34 a.2.1 fired 3250 rounds on (1) TRACK JUNCTION S6.d 90.35, (2) ROAD S.12 c 35–65 – c.65.50, (3) ROAD JUNCTION S11 d. 8.3, (4) TRACK JUNCTION S12 a. 60.15. 9 pm to 3.45 am. Amb.	

[illegible signature]

2353 Wt. W2544/1454 700,000 5/15 D. D. & L. A.D.S.S./Forms/C. 2118.

Instructions regarding War Diaries and Intelligence Summaries are contained in F. S. Regs., Part II. and the Staff Manual respectively. Title pages will be prepared in manuscript.

WAR DIARY
or
~~INTELLIGENCE SUMMARY~~.
(Erase heading not required.)

Army Form C. 2118.

Place	Date	Hour	Summary of Events and Information	Remarks and references to Appendices
			147 Machine Gun Company.	
RICHEBOURG.	6.5.17		No. 4 Section relieved No. 1 Section in "CENTRE" positions. AmB.	
	7.5.17		M.G. at EDWARD'S POST fired 3000 rounds on (1) LA TOURELLE CROSS ROADS, (2) DISTILLERY, (3) NORA TRENCH, (4) LA TOURELLE FARM, 10 pm – 12.30 am. MG. M.34 d.2.1 fired 3000 rounds on (1) FME DU BIEZ S12c. 15.25, (2) TRENCH JUNCTION S11d.45.10, (3) ROAD S12c 15.05, (4) TRAMWAY JUNCTION S12 b.5.7, during night. AmB.	
	8.5.17		In conjunction with Gas bombardment by 49. Division, 5 Company MGs. fired 25,250 rounds from the following positions:- M.34d.2.1, S.4.a.95.90, ALBERT ROAD, PIPE STREET, EDWARD'S POST. from 11 pm. (ZERO) onwards. AmB.	
	9.5.17		M.G. at M.34.d.2.1 fired 3125 rounds on (1) FME DU BIEZ, S.12.c 15.25, (2) TRACK. S.6.d.90.35, (3) HOUSE and TRAMWAY. S.12.b.25.90, (4) ROAD. S.12.c.5.9, 9 pm to 4 am. AmB.	
	10.5.17		M.G. at EDWARD'S POST fired 4250 rounds on (1) LA TOURELLE CROSS ROADS, (2) NORA TRENCH, (3) TRACK at LA TOULOTTE FARM, 9.30 pm to 11 pm and 3.15 am – 4.15 am.	AmB.
	11.5.17		No. 1 Section relieved No. 2 Section in the "LEFT" positions.	
			MG. at EDWARD'S POST fired 4300 rounds on (1) LA TOURELLE CROSS ROADS, (2) DISTILLERY, (3) NORA TRENCH, (4) LA TOULOTTE FARM, 9.30 pm – 11.45 pm and 3 am – 4 am. AmB.	

[signature]

2353 Wt. W2544/1454 700,000 5/15 D. D. & L. A.D.S.S./Forms/C. 2118.

Instructions regarding War Diaries and Intelligence Summaries are contained in F. S. Regs., Part II. and the Staff Manual respectively. Title pages will be prepared in manuscript.

WAR DIARY
or
~~INTELLIGENCE SUMMARY~~.
(Erase heading not required.)

Army Form C. 2118.

Place	Date	Hour	Summary of Events and Information	Remarks and references to Appendices
			14.7th Machine Gun Company	
RICHEBOURG	11.5.17		A.A. GUN. fired 750 rounds at 8.45 am. at hostile 'plane. When fire was opened it was observed to waver in its flight, and retired flying in a very erratic manner. AmB.	
	12.5.17		Work begun by No 1 Section on new dug-out for KINGS CROSS position. MG at EDWARDS POST fired 4000 rounds on LA TOURELLE CROSS ROADS, LA TOULOTTE FARM, DISTILLERY, NORA TRENCH, from 9.15 pm to 11.30 pm and 3. am to 4 am. AmB.	
	13.5.17		Nothing to report. AmB	
	14.5.17		No 2 Section relieved No 3 Section in the "RIGHT" positions. M.G at S.8d.9.6 fired (1) 750 rounds on MITZI TRENCH at 10pm – 11pm, (2) 1000 rounds on LA TOURELLE at 11pm – midnight, (3) 1250 rounds on ROAD and TRENCH JUNCTIONS from midnight to 2 am. (4) 1000 rounds on FME DU TOULOTTE from 2 am to 3.15 am, (5) 500 rounds on TRACKS from 3.15 am – 3.45 am. AmB.	
	15.5.17		MG. at S.8.d.9.6. fired (1) 450 rounds on SERPENT TRENCH from 10 pm to 10.30 pm, (2) 700 rounds on NORA TRENCH from 10.30 pm to 11 pm, (3) 600 rounds on DISTILLERY from 11 pm to 11.30 pm. AmB	

[illegible signature], Major

2353 Wt. W2544/1454 700,000 5/15 D. D. & L. A.D.S.S./Forms/C. 2118.

Instructions regarding War Diaries and Intelligence Summaries are contained in F. S. Regs., Part II. and the Staff Manual respectively. Title pages will be prepared in manuscript.

WAR DIARY
or
~~INTELLIGENCE SUMMARY~~.
(*Erase heading not required.*)

Army Form C. 2118.

Place	Date	Hour	Summary of Events and Information	Remarks and references to Appendices
			147th. Machine Gun Company.	
RICHEBOURG	16.5.17		MG. at S.8.d.9.6 fired (1) 1250 rounds on ENEMY BATTLN HQ from 9.30 pm to 10.30 pm, (2) 1000 rounds on MITZI TRENCH from 10.30 pm – midnight, (3) 1000 rounds on LA TOURELLE from midnight to 2.am, (4) 800 rounds on DISTILLERY from 2.am to 3.45 am. A.W.S.	
	17.5.17		MG. at S.8.d.9.6 fired (1) 1500 rounds on LA TOURELLE, 9.30 pm to 11.30 pm, (2) 1500 rounds MITZI TRENCH, 11.30 pm to 2.am, (3) 1125 rounds on DISTILLERY, 2 am – 3 am. The above firing was done in conjunction with the R.F.A. A.W.S.	
	18.5.17		No 3 Section relieved No 4 Section in the "CENTRE" positions. MG. at S.8.d.9.6 fired (1) 1000 rounds on NORA TRENCH, 9.30 pm to 10.30 pm (2) 1250 rounds on ROAD. 10.30 pm to midnight, (3) 950 rounds on LA TOURELLE midnight to 2.am, (4) 1000 rounds on ENEMY. HQ. 2.am to 3.45 am. A.W.S.	
	19.5.17		MG at S.8.d.9.6 fired (1) 1000 rounds on S.17.a.5.4, from 9.30 pm to 10.30 pm, (2) 1250 rounds on ST. STEPHEN'S WALK from 10.30 pm to 11.30 pm, (3) 1000 rounds on DISTILLERY from 11.30 pm to 1. am, (4) 1125 rounds on S.17.d.2.8 from 1.am to 2.30 am in conjuction with Artillery. A.W.S.	
	20.5.17		MG. at S.8.d.9.6 fired (1) 1250 rounds on NORA TRENCH, 9.30 pm to 11 pm, (2) 1000 rounds on LA TOURELLE. 11 pm – 12.30 am, (3) 500 rounds on S.17.b.3.9 from 12.30 am to 2 am. A.W.S.	[signature]

Army Form C. 2118.

Instructions regarding War Diaries and Intelligence Summaries are contained in F. S. Regs., Part II. and the Staff Manual respectively. Title pages will be prepared in manuscript.

WAR DIARY
or
~~INTELLIGENCE SUMMARY~~.
(Erase heading not required.)

Place	Date	Hour	Summary of Events and Information	Remarks and references to Appendices
			147th Machine Gun Company	
RICHEBOURG.	20.5.17		(1) 750 rounds on MITZI WALK, 2 am to 3.45 am. MG. at S.4.a.90.95 fired bursts of 100, 150 and 150 rounds at hostile 'plane which was prevented from crossing our lines. MG. at S.4.b.05.95 fired 1500 rounds on DUMPS and LA TOURELLE between 9.30 pm and 11.45 pm. AmS.	
	21.5.17		MG. at S.8.d.9.6 fired (1) 900 rounds on DISTILLERY, 9.30 pm – 11 pm, (2) 650 rounds on MITZI WALK, 11 pm to 12.30 am, (3) 750 rounds on ENEMY HQ, 12.30 am to 2 am, (4) 1250 rounds on TRACKS, 2 am – 3.30 am. MG. at S.4.a.90.95 fired bursts of 100 and 400 at hostile plane which turned back over its own lines. MG. at S.4.b.05.95 fired 2000 rounds traversing enemy trench RAILWAY passing through S.6.d, S.6.c, and S.12.a, 9.30 pm to 11.55 pm. AmS.	
	22.5.17		No 4 Section relieved No 1 Section in "LEFT" positions. M.G. at PIMPS. POST fired 2000 rounds on TRAMWAY behind BOIS DU BIEZ, 9.45 pm – 3 am. M.G at S.8.d.9.6. fired (1) 1000 rounds on MITZI WALK, 9.30 pm to 11 pm, (2) 950 rounds on LA TOURELLE, 11 pm to 12.30 am, (3) 1100 rounds on ROADS, 12.30 am to 2.30 am, (4) 550 rounds on ROADS, 2.30 am to 3.45 am. AmS.	
	23.5.17		MG. at S.8.d.9.6 fired (1) 950 rounds on ENEMY HQ, 9.45 pm to 11. pm.	[signature]

2353 Wt. W2544/1454 700,000 5/15 D. D. & L. A.D.S.S./Forms/C. 2118.

Instructions regarding War Diaries and Intelligence Summaries are contained in F. S. Regs., Part II. and the Staff Manual respectively. Title pages will be prepared in manuscript.

WAR DIARY
or
~~INTELLIGENCE SUMMARY~~.
(Erase heading not required.)

Army Form C. 2118.

Place	Date	Hour	Summary of Events and Information	Remarks and references to Appendices
			147th Machine Gun Company.–	
RICHEBOURG	23.5.17		(2) 1150 rounds on ROADS, 11pm – 12.45am, (3) 750 rounds on ROADS, 12.45am to 2.15 am, (4) 850 rounds on DISTILLERY, 2.15am to 3.45am. MG. at PIMPS POST fired 2250 rounds on BOIS DU BIEZ, 10pm to 2.am and 150 rounds at hostile 'plane at 6.10 pm whereupon he returned over his own line.	Am[illegible]
	24.5.17		Work begun by No 1 Section on dug-out for KINGS CROSS position completed by No 4 Section. Work begun by No 3 Section on Section HQ ORCHARD POST completed by No 2 Section. MG. at S.8d.9.6 fired (1) 800 rounds on ROADS, 9.30pm – 11pm, (2) 750 rounds on MITZI WALK, 11pm – 12.30am, (3) 1100 rounds on LA TOURELLE, 12.30am – 2.15am, (4) 1050 rounds on DISTILLERY, 2.15am – 3.45am. MG. at PIMPS POST fired 2000 rounds on BOIS DU BIEZ, 11.30pm – 3.30am, also 50 rounds on hostile plane, 7.40pm.	Am[illegible]
	25.5.17		MG at PIMPS POST fired 2250 rounds on BOIS DU BIEZ and LA TOURELLE, 10pm – 3.30am, and 750 rounds at hostile plane during the day. MG. at S.8.d.9 6 fired (1) 800 rounds on MITZI WALK	[illegible signature]

2353 Wt. W2344/1454 700,000 5/15 D. D. & L. A.D.S.S./Forms/C. 2118.

Instructions regarding War Diaries and Intelligence Summaries are contained in F. S. Regs., Part II. and the Staff Manual respectively. Title pages will be prepared in manuscript.

WAR DIARY
or
~~INTELLIGENCE SUMMARY.~~
(*Erase heading not required.*)

Army Form C. 2118.

Place	Date	Hour	Summary of Events and Information	Remarks and references to Appendices
			147 Machine Gun Company	
RICHEBOURG.	25.5.17		9.30 pm – 11 pm, (2) 750 rounds on ROADS, 11 pm to 12.30 am, (3) 600 rounds on ROADS, 12.30 am – 2 am, (4) 1150 rounds on ROADS. 2 am – 3.45 am. AmbS.	
	26.5.17		No 1 Section relieved No 2 Section in the "RIGHT" positions. MG. at S.8.d.9.6 fired (1) 500 rounds on S.17.a.85.60, 10 pm to 1 am, (2) 1000 rounds at DISTILLERY, 10.45 pm to 1.20 am, (3) 800 rounds on S.17.a.3.7. and 750 rounds on S.17.c.0.6. A.A. Gun fired 600 rounds on hostile plane at 6 am and 9.30 am. Aeroplane was driven back over his own lines. 2000 rounds were fired on BOIS DU BIEZ & LA TOURELLE, 9.30 pm and 1 am. AmbS.	
	27.5.17		MG. S.8.d.9.6 fired 3200 rounds on usual targets viz: roads & tracks. MG. at PIMPS POST fired 2500 rounds at BOIS DU BIEZ, ~~10 pm & 3.30 am~~ and LA TOURELLE, 10 pm – 3.30 am. AmbS.	
	28.5.17		MG at PIMPS POST fired 2500 rounds on BOIS DU BIEZ, 10 pm & 3.30 am in retaliation for enemy M.G. fire. MG at S.8.d.9.6 fired 2950 rounds on SHEPHERD'S REDOUBT and TRACKS, between 10 pm & 3 am. Two MGs moved to front line in connection with raid carried	

W. M. Sparrow(?) Major

2353 Wt. W2544/1454 700,000 5/15 D. D. & L. A.D.S.S./Forms/C. 2118.

Army Form C. 2118.

Instructions regarding War Diaries and Intelligence Summaries are contained in F. S. Regs., Part II. and the Staff Manual respectively. Title pages will be prepared in manuscript.

WAR DIARY
or
~~INTELLIGENCE SUMMARY~~.
(*Erase heading not required.*)

147 Machine Gun Company.

Place	Date	Hour	Summary of Events and Information	Remarks and references to Appendices
RICHEBOURG.	28.5.17		out by 7th West Riding Regiment. Guns were manned by No 3 Section. AmbS.	
	29.5.17		MG. at PIMPS POST fired 2.250 rounds on TRAMWAYS and TRACKS behind BOIS DU BIEZ between 9.30 pm + 3.30 am, in retaliation for enemy M.G. fire. MG at S.8.d.9.6 fired 2700 rounds on DISTILLERY, ROADS, + TRACKS, between 9.20 pm and 3. am. 147 Brigade relieved in line (FME DU BOIS SECTOR) by 1st Division, PORTUGESE. E.F, with the exception of M.G. COY. and T.M.B's who are to stay in until corresponding units of the Portugese E.F. are instructed. AmbS.	
	30.5.17		MG. at PIMPS POST fired 3000 rounds on LA TOURELLE, FME DU BIEZ, + LA BASSEE RD, in retaliation for hostile MG. fire, from 9.30 pm to 3.30 am, opening whenever hostile MG. fired. MG. at S.8.d.9.6 fired 3.020 rounds on SHEPHERDS REDOUBT and S.17.a.85.60 from 9.30 pm to 2 am. AmbS.	
	31.5.17		MG at PIMPS POST fired 3000 rounds on usual targets during night. MG. at S.8.d.9.6 fired 3000 rounds on usual targets, + in retaliation for enemy MG. fire during night. AmbS.	

2353 Wt. W2544/1454 700,000 5/15 D. D. & L. A.D.S.S./Forms/C. 2118.

Vol 18

Confidential War Diary.

147 th. Machine Gun Company.

30th June 1917.

[illegible signature]

Instructions regarding War Diaries and Intelligence Summaries are contained in F. S. Regs., Part II. and the Staff Manual respectively. Title pages will be prepared in manuscript.

WAR DIARY
or
~~INTELLIGENCE SUMMARY.~~

(Erase heading not required.)

Army Form C. 2118.

142. Machine Gun Coy.

Place	Date	Hour	Summary of Events and Information	Remarks and references to Appendices
FERME DU BOIS. Sector RICHEBOURG	1/6/17.		M.G at S.9.c.25.20 fired 750 rounds at hostile aeroplane over our lines and caused it to climb out of range. M.G at S.8.d.9.6 fired 2000 rounds intermittently 9.30pm - 1.30am on following points :- S.17.a.5.4, S.11.c.55.30 and S.17.c.0.6. M.G at PIMPS POST fired 3000 rounds on usual targets during night.	a.b.
-Ditto--	2/6/17.		M.G at PIMPS POST fired 1500 rounds on LA BASSEE ROAD, DISTILLERY, FERME DU BIEZ - 9.30pm to 3.30am. M.G at S.8.d.9.6 fired 2000 rounds at DISTILLERY and S.17.a.85.60 from 9.30pm to 1.0am.	a.b.
-Ditto-	3/6/17.		No 3 Section relieved No 4 Section in LEFT POSITIONS. M.G at S.9.c.25.20 fired 300 rounds at hostile aeroplane observing for heavy artillery, whereupon aeroplane climbed and returned to ~~xxx~~ own lines. M.G at S.8.d.9.6 fired 2000 rounds on S.17.b.30.95. M.G at PIMPS POST fired 2500 rounds on BOIS DU BIEZ and LA TOURELLE Cross Roads and FERME DU BIEZ 10.0pm to 2.30am.	a.b.
-Ditto-	4/6/17.		M.G at S.9.c.25.20 fired 100 rounds at enemy aeroplane at 10.0am. M.G at S.8.d.9.6 fired 2000 rounds on SHEPHERDS REDOUBT and S.17.a.30.05 9.30pm to 1.0am. M.G at PIMPS POST fired 3000 rounds on BOIS DU BIEZ, TOURELLE CROSS ROADS and FERME DU BIEZ.	a.b.
-Ditto-	5/6/17.		M.G at S.8.d.9.6 fired 1910 rounds on NITZI TRENCH and S.17.a.5.4 from 9.30pm to 12.30am. M.G at PIMPS POST fired 1500 rounds on BOIS DU BIEZ and TOURELLE CROSS ROADS, and FERME DU BIEZ from 10.15pm to 2.30am.	a.b.
-Ditto-	6/6/17.		M.G at S.8.d.9.6 fired 1850 rounds on DISTILLERY and S.17.a.85.60.. M.G at PIMPS POST fired 1500 rounds on BOIS DU BIEZ, LA TOURELLE CROSS ROADS and FERME DU BIEZ - 9.45pm to 2.0am. No 1 Section Casualties , 1 man wounded.	a.b.

2353 Wt. W2544/1454 700,000 5/15 D. D. & L. A.D.S.S./Forms/C. 2118.

Instructions regarding War Diaries and Intelligence Summaries are contained in F. S. Regs., Part II. and the Staff Manual respectively. Title pages will be prepared in manuscript.

Army Form C. 2118.

WAR DIARY
or
~~INTELLIGENCE~~ SUMMARY.
(Erase heading not required.)

Place	Date	Hour	Summary of Events and Information 144th Machine Gun Coy	Remarks and references to Appendices
FERME DU BOIS Sector RICHEBOURG.	7/6/17.		No 4 Section relieved No 1 Section in RIGHT POSITIONS. M.G at PIMPS POST fired 1500 rounds on BOIS DU BIEZ and LA TOURELLIE CROSS ROADS - 10.15pm to 2.30pm. 750 rounds fired at hostile aeroplanes during day. No 4 Section A.A Gun fired 200 rounds -9.0am to 10.30am, 200 rounds fired on MITZI and NORA trenches - 10.30pm to 1.30am.	
-Ditto-	8/6/17.		M.G at PIMPS POST fired 1500 rounds on BOIS DU BIEZ, LATOURELLIE CROSS ROADS and FERME DU BIEZ - 10.30pm to 2.30am. M.G at S.8.d.9.6 fired 1500 rounds on NORA & MITZI TRENCHES,10.30pm to 1.0am.	
-Ditto-	9/6/17.		M.G at PIMPS POST fired 1500 rounds on BOIS DU BIEZ, 10.0pm to 11.15pm . M.G at S.8.d.9.6 fired 1500 rounds on SHEPHERDS REDOUBT & QUINQUE RUE 11.0pm to 1.0am.	
-Ditto-	10/6/17.		No 3 Section gun at PIMPS POST fired 1500 rounds on BOIS DU BIEZ, LA TOURELLIE CROSS ROADS and FERME DU BIEZ from 10.0pm to 2.30am	
-Ditto-	11/6/17.		No 3 Sections' gun at PIMPS POST fired 3000 rounds at BOIS DU BIEZ and SHEPHERDS REDOUBT, LA TOURELLIE CROSS ROADS,and FERME DU BIEZ from 10.0pm to 3.0am.	
Ditto	12/6/17.		No 3 Sections' gun at PIMPS POST fired 2000 rounds on BOIS DU BIEZ, LA TOURELLIE CROSS ROADS and FERME DU BIEZ from 9.30am to 2.30am.	
-Ditto-	13/6/17.		Gun at PIMPS POST fired 2500 rounds at BOIS DU BIEZ, LA TOURELLIE CROSS ROADS and FERME DU BIEZ from 10.0pm to 2.30am.	
-Ditto-	14/6/17.		Gun at PIMPS POST fired 3500 rounds at SHEPHERDS REDOUBT,and on the back of the BOIS DU BIEZ from 9.50pm to 2.50am. No 4 Section's gun near ORCHARDS POST fired 1000 rounds on MITZI TRENCH from 9.50pm to 11.45pm.	

2353 Wt. W2544/1454 700,000 5/15 D. D. & L. A.D.S.S./Forms/C. 2118.

Instructions regarding War Diaries and Intelligence Summaries are contained in F. S. Regs., Part II. and the Staff Manual respectively. Title pages will be prepared in manuscript.

WAR DIARY
or
~~INTELLIGENCE SUMMARY.~~
(Erase heading not required.)

Army Form C. 2118.

144. Machine Gun Coy

Place	Date	Hour	Summary of Events and Information	Remarks and references to Appendices
FERME DU BOIS.	15/6/17.		All quiet - Machine gun fire NIL.	
-Ditto-	16/6/17.		The Company were relieved in the line by the 199th M.G.Coy. Relief complete by 12.0 noon. When relieved the Company were concentrated at ZELOBES.	
ZELOBES.	17/6/17.		In rest at ZELOBES - Cleaning equipment etc., preparatory to next move.	
ZELOBES & NOYELLES.	18/6/17.		Company marched from ZELOBES to billets in NOYELLES, starting at 5.0am arriving at 9.0am. Section Officers went round the new line.	
ST ELIE Sector LOOS.	19/6/17.		The Company relieved the 71st Machine Gun Company in the ST ELIE Sector. Sections disposed of as follows:- No 1 Section - VILLAGE LINE. -- No 2 Section RIGHT Sector. No 3 Section - Reserve at Headquarters -- No 4 Section LEFT Sector. Company Headquarters at BREWERY in VERMELLES. Relief complete by Midnight. Indirect fire was done by No 1 Section from Gun position at G.16.a.3.9, 950 rounds being fired at a T.M position at G.6.c.08.04 from 8.20pm to 12.15am	
-Ditto-	20/6/17.		Heavy enemy Trench Mortar activity in RIGHT & LEFT Sectors necessitating the removal of the gun at FARMERS LANE in the LEFT Sector to STANSFIELD RD. No 1 Section gun fired at G.16.a.8.9 fired 800 rounds at G.12.a.8.3 to G.12.c.0.4 from 8.30pm to 11.0pm.	
-Ditto-	21/6/17.		Enemy lightly shelled junction of CHAPEL ALLEY and O.B.1 with 4.2" shells for about half an hour at Noon, otherwise all quiet. No 1 Section gun at G.16.a.8.9 fired 1090 rounds on enemy T.M emplacement in QUARRIES at G.12.a from 8.30pm to 1.0am.	
-Ditto-	22/6/17.		Situation quiet. Machine Gun fire NIL.	

Instructions regarding War Diaries and Intelligence Summaries are contained in F. S. Regs., Part II. and the Staff Manual respectively. Title pages will be prepared in manuscript.

WAR DIARY
or
~~INTELLIGENCE SUMMARY.~~
(Erase heading not required.)

Army Form C. 2118.

147 Machine Gun Coy

Place	Date	Hour	Summary of Events and Information	Remarks and references to Appendices
ST ELIE Sector LOOS.	23/6/17.		Situation quiet. - No 1 Section gun at G.11.c.70.32 fired 250 rounds on PUITS No 13 and Tracks at H.7.b.15.58 to H.7.b.85.28 from 4.30pm to 6.0pm, and 500 rounds on Trench Railway running from G.12.b.3.6 to G.12.b.7.7 from 10.0pm to 12.30am.	
-Ditto-	24/6/17.		Co-operated with the 16th Brigade on our right who did a raid, with barrage fire to the N.E of the raided area. Zero hour 9.0pm. Dispositions of guns as follows:- Two guns at R.55 fired 2500 rounds each on Trench from H.7.a.10.10 to H.7.c.6.8 Two guns at R.53.a fired 2500 rounds each on these targets H.7.d.25.85 to H.7.d.10.15 and H.13.b.55.35. Three guns at R.53 fired 2500 rounds on these targets : H.7.d.25.30 to H.13.b.75.90. - H.7.c.90.62 to H.7.d.25.36, and H.7.c.38.46 to H.7.c.99.60. Fire was maintained from Zero to Zero plus 50 minutes. These guns were acting under the O.C 9th M.G.Squadron who was i/c of M.G arrangements for the raid.	
-Ditto-	25/6/17.		Quiet day. No 4 Sections' gun at R.56 fired 300 rounds at hostile aircraft. No 1 Sections' guns at G.11.c.70.43 fired 750 rounds on hostile aircraft at 5.0pm. Also No 1 Sections' gun at G.10.c.29.47 fired 1000 rounds on Trench Railway running from G.5.d.70.32 to G.6.c.27.90 from 9.30pm to 12.15am.	
-Ditto-	26/6/17.		Quiet day. No 3 Section with two guns took up positions in Gun Trench N.of LOOS at about 8.0pm in order to bring fire to bear during the nights 26/27th, and 27/28th inst on the area enclosed by : H.31.d.35.50 - H.31.b.35.00 H.32.c.50.50 - ,H.32.a.50.50, in conjunction with operations further South. Firing for nights 26/27th from position at G.30.c.2.7 was 9000 rounds on area given from 10.15pm to 3.30am No 1 Sections' gun at G.10.c.29.47 fired 1000 rounds on enemy Trench Mortar emplacements at G.12.a.42.58, G.12.a.76.38 and G.12.a.80.20.	

Army Form C. 2118.

WAR DIARY
or
~~INTELLIGENCE SUMMARY.~~
(Erase heading not required.)

Instructions regarding War Diaries and Intelligence Summaries are contained in F. S. Regs., Part II. and the Staff Manual respectively. Title pages will be prepared in manuscript.

144. Machine Gun Coy.

Place	Date	Hour	Summary of Events and Information	Remarks and references to Appendices
ST ELIE Sector LOOS.	27/6/17.		At 3.5am the enemy opened a barrage of Trench Mortars and shells of all calibres in the neighbourhood of K.POST in the RIGHT Sector. The barrage lasted 40 minutes during which time the guns at DUDLEY DUMP and ST GEORGE'S POST were dismounted. When the barrage lifted the guns were immediately mounted, but the left gun at DUDLEY DUMP had to be withdrawn again for 5 minutes owing to our own shells falling short. The enemy then raided the front line, and all four guns got into actio the left two sweeping the enemy front line while the DUDLEY DUMP gun got a target at about G.12.a.5.8 where about six enemy men were seen returning to their own lines. It is believed casualties were inflicted, though observation was difficult. The guns were in action for 35 minutes and fired 10950 rounds. At the same time two of No 1 Sections guns at G.10.c.29.47 and G.16.a.39 put a barrage on the QUARRIES, firing 1250 & 1750 rounds respectively. No 3 Section at LOOS carried out their second nights' firing. 9000 round being fired by the two guns from 10 pm to 3.0am on the same targets.	KBB
ST ELIE Sector LOOS.	28/6/17.		No 3 Section returned from LOOS at 4.0am to Coy Headquarters. Bombardment at 7.10pm in conjunction with operations further South. Very slight retaliation. No 1 Sections' gun at G.11.c.72232 fired 430 rounds on light railway G.12.c.3.6 to G.12.c.7.7 from 10pm to 12.5am, and the gun at G.10.c.22 fired 980 rounds at T.M's in Quarries from 7.40pm to 9.10pm.	KBB
-ditto-	29/6/17.		M.G at G.16.a.80.85 fired 1250 rounds on Tramway at G.12.a.3.6 & A78 10.20pm to 12 Midnight.	KBB
NOYELLES.	30/6/17.		The Company were relieved in the ST ELIE Sector by the 71st M.G.Coy. Relief complete by 3.0pm. After relief Company proceeded to NOYELLES to billets for the night.	KBB

2353 Wt. W2544/1454 700,000 5/15 D. D. & L. A.D.S.S./Forms/C. 2118.

Vol 19

147th MACHINE GUN COMPANY.
****

C O N F I D E N T I A L.
****

WAR DIARY.
****

for JULY 1917.
****

[signature] Capt
147 Machine Gun Coy.

147th MACHINE GUN COMPANY.

CONFIDENTIAL.

WAR DIARY.

for

July. 1917.

Army Form C. 2118.

WAR DIARY
or
INTELLIGENCE SUMMARY.
(Erase heading not required.)

Instructions regarding War Diaries and Intelligence Summaries are contained in F. S. Regs., Part II. and the Staff Manual respectively. Title pages will be prepared in manuscript.

Place	Date	Hour	Summary of Events and Information	Remarks and references to Appendices
			147th MACHINE GUN COMPANY.	
NOYELLES.	1/7/17.		Company left NOYELLES for BETHUNE to billets for the night.	a.b.
BETHUNE.	2.7.17.		Company left BETHUNE at 4.30am, arriving at REGNIER LE CLERE near MERVILLE at 10.0am.	a.b.
REGNIER LE CLERE	3/7/17.		Company training 9.30am to 1.0pm.	a.b.
" "	4/7/17.		Company training 9.30am to 1.0pm & bathing for men at 6.0pm.	a.b.
" "	5/7/17.		--- ditto ---	a.b.
" "	6/7/17.		--- ditto ---	a.b.
" "	7/7/17.		Company training 9.30am to 12 Noon. Brigade Sports at PAGAUT (Prize won by Transport.	a.b.
" "	8/7/17.		Company training 9.30am to 1.0pm.	a.b.
" "	9/7/17.		--- ditto ---	a.b.
" "	10/7/17.		--- ditto ---	a.b.
" "	11/7/17.		--- ditto ---	a.b.
" "	12/7/17.		--- ditto --- & Cleaning up preparatory to moving.	a.b.
" "	13/7/17.		Company left billets 3.0am, entrained at MERVILLE, left at 5.0am, arrived DUNKIRK at 12 Midday, and proceeded to camp at ST POL. Half of the men in tents, and remainder bivouacing.	a.b.
DUNKIRK.	14/7/17.		Training 9.30am to 1.0pm. Bathing parade at 3.0pm.	a.b.
"	15/7/17.		Church parade 9.30am. Training 11.0am to 1.0pm.	a.b.

[illegible] Capt
Comd 147 M.G. Coy

A5834 Wt W4973/M687 750,000 8/16 D. D. & L. Ltd. Forms/C.2118/13.

Instructions regarding War Diaries and Intelligence Summaries are contained in F. S. Regs., Part II. and the Staff Manual respectively. Title pages will be prepared in manuscript.

WAR DIARY
or
~~INTELLIGENCE SUMMARY.~~
(Erase heading not required.)

Army Form C. 2118.

Place	Date	Hour	Summary of Events and Information	Remarks and references to Appendices
			147th MACHINE GUN COMPANY.	
DUNKIRK.	16/7/17.		Company training.	
DUNKIRK	17/7/17.		Cleaning up preparatory to moving. O.C. Company (Major W.J.M.SPROULLE) lef to be D.M.G.O.	
BRAY DUNES.	18/7/17.		Company left Camp at 4.15am and marched to BRAY DUNES to billets, arriving 8.10am.	
" "	19/7/17.		Move orders cancelled at Midnight, stayed in billets all day. Captain MUHLIG.M.C. from the 199th M.G.Coy assumed Command of the Company.	
GHYVELDE.	20/7/17.		Left BRAY DUNES 7.30am and marched to GHYVELDE to billets, arriving at 8.30 am.	
" "	21/7/17.		Company training 8.30am to 1.30pm - 2.30pm to 4.30pm - 6.0pm to 7.0pm.	
" "	22/7/17.		Church parade with the 4th West Riding Regt.	
" "	23/7/17.		Company training.	
" "	24/7/17.		--- ditto ---	
" "	25/7/17.		Company training. 40 men from 147th M.G.Coy attached (pro.tem:) to 148th Machine Gun Company.	
" "	26/7/17.		Company training.	
" "	27/7/17.		Company training.	
" "	28/7/17.		Company training.	

A5834 Wt. W4973/M687 750,000 8/16 D. D. & L. Ltd. Forms/C.2118/13.

Army Form C. 2118.

WAR DIARY
or
~~INTELLIGENCE SUMMARY.~~
(Erase heading not required.)

Instructions regarding War Diaries and Intelligence Summaries are contained in F. S. Regs., Part II. and the Staff Manual respectively. Title pages will be prepared in manuscript.

Place	Date	Hour	Summary of Events and Information	Remarks and references to Appendices
			147th MACHINE GUN COMPANY. ***************************	
GHYVELDE.	29.7.17.		Nos 1 & 3 Sections with their respective Transport moved to billets at OOST DUNKERQUE.	A.B.
" " "	30.7.17.		Company Training.	A.B.
" " "	31.7.17.		Nos 2 & 4 Sections took over Anti-aircraft Defence positions from the 97th Machine Gun Company at following places: MALO BAINS. COXYDE. AVE CAPELLE. FURNES. Company Headquarters remained at GHYVELDE.	A.B.

In the Field
31-7-17

J Muckley Capt
Commdg 147 M.G. Coy.

A5834 Wt. W4973/M687 750,000 8/16 D. D. & L. Ltd. Forms/C.2118/13.

Vol 20

147th MACHINE GUN COMPANY.

C O N F I D E N T I A L.

W A R D I A R Y.

for AUGUST 1917.

PAGE. I

Instructions regarding War Diaries and Intelligence Summaries are contained in F. S. Regs., Part II. and the Staff Manual respectively. Title pages will be prepared in manuscript.

WAR DIARY ~~or INTELLIGENCE SUMMARY.~~ of 144th Machine Gun Company for AUGUST 1917

(Erase heading not required.)

Army Form C. 2118.

Place	Date	~~Hour~~ Day	Summary of Events and Information	Remarks and references to Appendices
GHYVELDE	31/7/17	Tues	A fine day, inclined to rain, strong breeze from sea throughout day. Heavy Rain & wind throughout the night. O.C. Coy to Hd Qrs 94th M.G. Coy thence round Anti Aircraft defences, returned to Coy Hd Qrs. at 10.30 am. Issued orders for Sections who left for various destinations at 1 pm. Relief of 94th Coy reported complete by 6 p.m. Coy Hd Qrs. moved to BRAY DUNES during afternoon but owing to lack of billeting accommodation had to return to Ghyvelde. A quiet 24 hours in the Billeting Area. Sick Nil Casualties Nil. Strength of Coy 11 Offrs 211 other Rks (including 32 attached) (2 Field Amb)	
Hd Quarters GHYVELDE.	1/8/17	Wed.	A foul day, heavy rain & wind throughout the day. Officers on Strength of Company 1st August 1917 as follows. CAPT. J. MUNRO M.C. East Yorkshire Regt. Commanding Coy. Lieut A B Selman. 1/4th GLOUCESTER Regt. 2/in Command. CAPT C C BAIN. 1/4th West Riding Regt. -- No 4 Section. -- HANAGAN M. G. Corps. Sub Sect Offr No 2 LIEUT BOXER. M. G. Corps. -- No 3 -- -- 1. S. PHILLIPS M. G. Corps -- 4 (Lewis) -- HALL. M. G. Corps -- No 2 -- 2/Lt. COATES M. G. Corps -- 3. 2/Lieut SMITH M. G. Corps -- No 1 -- -- Slater R. G. Artillery -- 1. LIEUT G.C. FOULDS 1/6 West Rid. Regt Transport Offr. Distribution of Company. Coy Head Quarters GHYVELDE. Nos 1 + 2 Sections Oost DUNKERQUE. 1 Sub Section No 2. at St. IDESBALDS. 1 Sub Section No 2 at AVE CAPELLE. 1 Sub Section No 4. COXYDE. 1 Sub Section No 4 at MALO BAINS TERMINUS. 40 GUNNERS in LOMBARDZYDE SECTOR Trenches under command of O.C. 148 M.G. Coy. During day O.C. Coy visited all detachments, found all well & comfortable. During evening were warned to vacate present Coy Hd Qrs on the 2nd. Lieut Selman to BRAY DUNES. Re Billets.	

2353 Wt. W5432/1454 700,000 5/15 D. D. & L. A.D.S.S./Forms/C. 2118.

Page 2.

Instructions regarding War Diaries and Intelligence Summaries are contained in F. S. Regs., Part II. and the Staff Manual respectively. Title pages will be prepared in manuscript.

WAR DIARY of. 144th MACHINE GUN COMPANY for AUGUST. 1914.

~~or INTELLIGENCE SUMMARY.~~

(Erase heading not required.)

Army Form C. 2118.

Place	Date	~~Hour~~ Day	Summary of Events and Information	Remarks and references to Appendices
	1/8/14	Contd.	Promised Billet after a trying time walking about the area. Heavy rain throughout the night. Brigade orderly arrived at midnight with orders for a further distribution of the Company. A quiet 24 hours in the billet area. Sick Nil, Casualties Nil. Strength of Company 11 Offrs 211 other Ranks (2 Field Amb)	[illegible]
Hd Qrs GHYVELDE	2/8/14	Thurs.	Another rotten day, rain & wind throughout the day. During the forenoon 2/Lt COATES & a sub section of No 3 Section moved from OOST DUNKERQUE to Railhead N.W. of ADINKERQUE for the purpose of defending Ammn dumps from hostile aircraft. 6 Guns were ordered to move from OOST DUNKERQUE to BRAY DUNES to R.F.C. School, this move was cancelled at noon. O.C. Coy to Bde Hd Qrs. thence to OOST DUNKERQUE received Warning order to prepare to relieve the 199 Inf Brig in the LOMBARTZYDE Sector trenches. Coy Hd Qrs moved to BRAY DUNES during afternoon. A quiet 24 hours in billeting area. Sick Nil, Casualties Nil. Strength of Company 11 officers 211 other Ranks (2 F.A)	[illegible]
Hd Quarters BRAY DUNES	3/8/14	Frid.	Another bad day, wind & rain continue. Company still engaged on Coast Defences. Inf Battn of Brig & T.M.B. moved into line LOMBARTZYDE Section in relief of 199th Inf Brig. Bde Hd Qrs situated in NIEUPORT. A quiet 24 hours in billet areas. Sick Nil. Casualties Nil. Strength of Company 11 Offrs 211 O.R. (2 Field Ambulances)	[illegible]
Hd Quarters BRAY DUNES	4/8/14	Sat.	Another bad day, rain & wind continue throughout the day. Company paid out during the day. O.C. Coy visited ADINKERKE, found 1st Boxes & remainder of No 3 Section had arrived from OOST DUNKERQUE. Arrangements made for protection of Ammunition Dump at Sq W26 Central. A quiet 24 hours in Billeting area. Sick One O.R. (2 F.A) Casualties Nil. Strength of Company 11 Offs 211 other Ranks (3 Field Amb) 1 Off G.H.Q. School M.G. 1 Other Rk Same. 1 O.R. Leave U.K. 40 O.R. with 148 M.G. Coy. Remainder present with Coy.	[illegible]

2353 Wt. W2544/1454 700,000 5/15 D. D. & L. A.D.S.S./Forms/C. 2118.

Page 3.

Instructions regarding War Diaries and Intelligence Summaries are contained in F. S. Regs., Part II. and the Staff Manual respectively. Title pages will be prepared in manuscript.

WAR DIARY of 144 MACHINE GUN COMPANY

or

~~INTELLIGENCE SUMMARY.~~

(Erase heading not required.)

for AUGUST 1914

Army Form C. 2118.

Place	Date	~~Hour~~ Day	Summary of Events and Information	Remarks and references to Appendices
Hd Qrs BRAY DUNES	5/8/14	Sunday	A fine day, warm & bright. Divine Service for Hd Qrs with 2/Scottish Rifles during the forenoon. During the afternoon O.C. visited three sections at ADINKERQUE, found them just settling down in their new positions. A heavy mist during the night. A quiet 24 hours in Billeting area. Sick Nil. Casualties Nil. Strength of Coy 11 Offrs 211 other Rks. (3 Field Amb)	JMcapt
Hd Qrs BRAY DUNES	6/8/14	Monday	A fine day, O.C. Coy in company with D.M.G.O. visited all detachments found all correct. Returned to Coy Hd Qrs about 3pm. O.C. Coy attended Anti Aircraft school lecture during the afternoon. A quiet 24 hours in billet area. Sick Nil, Casualties Nil, Strength of Coy 11 Offrs 211 other Rks. (3 F.A. 32 attached from Battns)	JMcapt
Hd Qrs BRAY DUNES	7/8/14.	Tuesday	A fine day. Received news that the men attached to 148 Coy were out the line & resting, forwarded their valises to them. Pte WAITE attached from 6th W.R.R. to hospital. Struck off strength. During afternoon O.C. attended course of instruction in A.A duties. 2/Lt SMITH reported from Oost DUNKERQUE to Coy Hd Qrs. 2/Lt SLATER to Oost DUNKERQUE to command section whilst Smith is on leave to U.K. Visited by D.M.G.O. during forenoon & evening. Issued & forwarded Standing Orders to all Anti Aircraft Positions. A quiet & uneventful 24 hours in the Billet area. Sick One. Casualties Nil. Strength of Company 11 Offrs 210 Other Rks (31 attached from Battns)	JMcapt
Hd QUARTERS BRAY DUNES	8/8/14	Wed.	A fine day. 2/Lt Smith & Pte Mellor to XV Corps Reinforcement Camp en Route leave to U.K. Heavy storm, wind & rain during the night. Commenced fitting limbers with Racks to take Water Tins. During the day the men attached to 148 M.G.Coy, rejoined the company from COXYDE BAIN. O.C. 148 Coy reports that they done very well. Six were admitted to F.A. during the period. A quiet 24 hours in the Billet area. Sick Nil, Casualties Nil, Strength of Company 11 officers 210 other Ranks.	JMcapt

Page 14.

Instructions regarding War Diaries and Intelligence Summaries are contained in F. S. Regs., Part II. and the Staff Manual respectively. Title pages will be prepared in manuscript.

WAR DIARY of 144 MACHINE GUN COMPANY

~~or~~ ~~INTELLIGENCE SUMMARY.~~

(Erase heading not required.)

for AUGUST. 1914.

Army Form C. 2118.

Place	Date	~~Hour~~ Day	Summary of Events and Information	Remarks and references to Appendices
HD QUARTERS. BRAY DUNES	9/8/14	Thurs.	A fine day, clear & warm. 2/Lt Coates to Coxyde to take charge of Sub Section. Visited by D.M.G.O. during the afternoon. A quiet, uneventful 24 hours at all Company Posts. O.C. Coy visited ADENKERQUE Section during evening. Sick Nil Casualties Nil. Strength of Company 11 offs 210 other Ranks. (31 attached from Battns)	Jmcapt
HD QUARTERS. BRAY DUNES	10/8/14	Friday	A fine day, warm & bright. Maj Sproule D.M.G.O. to leave, C.O. becomes acting D.M.G.O. during his absence. Received orders re move during the night. A quiet uneventful 24 hours in Billet Area. Sick Nil Casualties Nil. Strength of Coy 11 offs 210 OR	Jmcapt
HD QUARTERS BRAY DUNES	11/8/14	Sat.	A fair day, showers during forenoon. Vet offr inspection of animals during afternoon, all correct. Stores partly moved to Oost Dunkirk during day. Reconnoitring parties from units relieving sections visited their posts. A quiet 24 hours. Sick Nil. Casualties Nil. Strength of Coy 11 offs (1 leave, 1 C of Instn) 209 other Rks (2 leave, 2 Course of Inst. + 6 F.A.)	Jmcapt
OOST DUNKIRK	12/8/14	Sunday	A fine day, warm & bright. Aerial activity during the day. Coy Hd Qrs left Bray DUNES at 9.30am. arrived Oost Dunkirk at 12 noon. During the day the company was relieved on A.A. defence duties by Lewis Gun Sections from the 32nd, 33rd, 49th & 66th Divisions. Relief was completed by 12 noon, with the exception of the 66th Div relief at Coxyde Dump. Relief was eventually completed by 12 m.n. Capt C W C Bann, C.S.M. Mitchell & Sgt Wheatcroft to AA Course with R.F.C. Hostile shelling of Oost Dunkirk was continual throughout the day. Reinforcement of 4 Ptes joined from Base depot, posted to No 2 Section. Pt Morris to C.C.S. Pt Goulden to C.R.S. Visited by O.C. 148 M.G. Coy during afternoon & relief arrangements made. Sick Nil. Casualties Nil, Strength of Company 11 offs (1 leave, 1 Course of Instruction) 212 other Ranks (2 leave, 2 Course of Instn, & 4 Field Amb).	Jmcapt

2353 Wt. W2544/1454 700,000 5/15 D. D. & L. A.D.S.S./Forms/C. 2118.

Page ~~5~~.

Instructions regarding War Diaries and Intelligence Summaries are contained in F. S. Regs., Part II. and the Staff Manual respectively. Title pages will be prepared in manuscript.

WAR DIARY of 147 Machine Gun Company

~~or INTELLIGENCE SUMMARY.~~

(Erase heading not required.)

Army Form C. 2118.

for August 1917

Place	Date	Day	Summary of Events and Information	Remarks and references to Appendices
Oost Dunkirk	13/8/17	Monday	A fine day, warm & bright. Aerial activity, hostile & friendly throughout the day. O.C. Coy met O.C. 148 M.G. Coy & reconnoitred the M.G. Coast Defences in view of taking over same. Company employed cleaning up during the day. Lt Sellman to Bde Hd Qrs. NIEUPORT re case of Pte Mitchell. A quiet uneventful 24 hours. Sick Nil, Casualties Nil, Strength of Company 11 Offrs (1 leave 2 C of Instn) 211 Other Rks (4 leave, 4 sick, 4 Class of Instn)	[illegible]
Oost Dunkirk	14/8/17	Tues.	A fine day, rain during afternoon. The Company relieved 148 M.G. Coy in the Coast Defences (Forward Area) relief commenced at 9 am, completed at 6.30 am. Coy Hd Qrs moved to COXYDE BAINS during morning. Disposition of Coy as follows. No 1 Section. Coast defences Nieuport Bain area, No 2 Section Oost Dunkirk area, No 3 Section Coxyde Bains area No 4 Section (less 1 S. Sect) St IDESBALDE area. Coy Hd Qrs, Transport & 1 Sub Sect No 4 at COXYDE BAIN. During the relief of NIEUPORT SECTOR Gas shells were fired by the enemy, with result that the forward sub section of 148 Coy were gassed & became casualties. O.C. Coy visited Hd Qrs 194th Inf Bde, during afternoon, saw Bde Major re stores etc & work on defences O.C. Coy reconnoitred No 3 & 4 Section areas during the evening. A quiet uneventful 24 hours. A few hostile shells about the Hd Qrs area during the night, no damage done. Sick Nil Casualties Nil Strength of Coy 11 Offrs 211 Other Rks (4 L.a.)	[illegible]
Coast Defences Nieuport Bains – St. Idesbalde	15/8/17	Wed.	A fine day, showers of rain during the forenoon. During early hours of the morning several hostile aeroplanes flew over the area, bomb dropping at various points. They were driven off by A A Fire, one being brought down in flames N.E. of Oost Dunkirk. O.C. Coy reconnoitred forward sections during forenoon, found all correct & quiet. During the night carried out experiment with Tracer Ammn, Capt Bain, C.S.M. & 1 Sgt rejoined from A A Course during the afternoon. Pte Mitchell released to duty under Suspension of Sentence Act. A quiet uneventful 24 hours. Sick Nil. Casualties Nil. Strength of Company 11 Offrs 211 other Ranks (includes 31 from Bns attached	[illegible]

2353 Wt. W2544/1454 700,000 5/15 D. D. & L. A.D.S.S./Forms/C. 2118.

PAGE 6.

Instructions regarding War Diaries and Intelligence Summaries are contained in F. S. Regs., Part II. and the Staff Manual respectively. Title pages will be prepared in manuscript.

WAR DIARY of 147. MACHINE GUN COMPANY for AUGUST. 1914

~~or INTELLIGENCE SUMMARY.~~

(Erase heading not required.)

Army Form C. 2118.

Place	Date	~~Hour~~ Day	Summary of Events and Information	Remarks and references to Appendices
COAST DEFENCES NIEUPORT - BAINS - ST IDESBALDE	16/8/14	Thurs	A fine day, cool breeze all day. O C Coy to Brig Hd Qrs 197 Brig during forenoon re work on Coast Defences & Shelter to Hd Qrs 199 M G Coy at COXYDE. During the night the 147 IB was relieved in the LOMBARTZYDE Sector by the 19th Inf Bde previous to taking over the Coast defences (Forward area). A quiet uneventful 24 hours in whole area, except slight shelling of Section at NIEUPORT BAINS. Sick Nil. Casualties Nil. Strength of Coy 11 offs 211 other Ranks	[signature]
COAST Defences NIEUPORT BAINS - ST IDESBALDE	17/8/14	Frid.	A fine day, cool breeze throughout day, O C Coy visited all sections in Forward area, found all correct, & improvements to defences being carried out. Hostile aerial activity about Coy Hd Qrs during early hours of morning. Hostile shelling of area during forenoon & a desultory shelling of Hd Qr area throughout the night which was very worrying especially to the Transport. 2 N Cos to Div Gas School for Trg as Coy Gas N C Os. O.C Coy to Brig Hd Qrs during evening. Sick Nil, Casualties Nil. Strength of Company 11 offs (1 Leave 1 Course of Inst) 211 other Ranks (4 F.A., 4 C. of I., 4 Leave, 199 actually present with Coy	[signature]
COAST Defences NIEUPORT BAINS - ST IDESBALDE	18/8/14	Saturday	A fine day, cool & bright. O C Coy visited all Guns in the Line, found all correct. O C Visited Bde Hd Qrs during the evening, all out, so saw nobody. A quiet uneventful 24 hrs in area, except for a slight hostile shelling of Coy Hd Qrs during the early hours. Sick Nil. Casualties Nil. Strength of Coy 11 offs 211 other Ranks.	[signature]
COAST Defences NIEUPORT BAINS - ST IDESBALDE	19/8/14	Sunday	A fine day, cool & bright. Reserve Section to Divine Service during forenoon. O.C. Coy visited forward guns of No 1. also went to Brig Hd Qrs, saw G.O.C. Bde. A quiet uneventful 24 hours, ~~except~~ except for hostile shelling near forward guns, with what were afterwards discovered to be 42 Cm shells. Sick Nil, Casualties Nil, Strength of Coy 11 offs 211 other Rks	[signature]
COAST Defences NIEUPORT BAINS - ST IDESBALDE	20/8/14	Monday	A fine day. Lt Hall relieved Lt HARAGHAN in Right Centre Sector during forenoon. Sub Sect No 4 under Capt Bain relieved Sub Section No 1 under Lt White on Right Sector during the night. Relief completed 12 m n. A quiet uneventful 24 hours in area. Sick Nil Casualties Nil. Strength of Company 11 offs 211 other Ranks. (4 Field Ambulance)	[signature]

2353 Wt. W2544/1454 700,000 5/15 D. D. & L. A.D.S.S./Forms/C. 2118.

Page 4

Instructions regarding War Diaries and Intelligence Summaries are contained in F. S. Regs., Part II. and the Staff Manual respectively. Title pages will be prepared in manuscript.

WAR DIARY of 144 Machine Gun Company
or
~~INTELLIGENCE SUMMARY.~~
(Erase heading not required.)
for AUGUST 1914.

Army Form C. 2118.

Place	Date	~~Hour~~ Day	Summary of Events and Information	Remarks and references to Appendices
Coast Defences Nieuport Bains – St Idesbalde	21/8/14	Tues	A fine day. Hostile aerial activity throughout early hours of morning. O C Coy visited all posts during the forenoon found all correct. Ptes Hacket & Wray to Field Amb. Sick. Sub Section of No 1 Section relieved the Sub Section of No 4 at St Idesbalde. Section at Nieuport Bains heavily shelled throughout the night very little damage done. Otherwise a quiet uneventful 24 hrs. Sick 2, Casualties Nil, Strength of Coy 11 Offrs 213 Other Ranks (Distribution of Personnel Offrs 9 Present 1 leave 1 C of I. Other Rks 194 Present 7 leave 6 Sick 6 Cys)	[signature]
Coast Defences Nieuport Bains – St Idesbalde	22/8/14	Wed	A fine day. Artillery both sides active during early hours of morning. O C Coy visited & Right Section Guns during the forenoon. Lt Selman visited 2 left Section Guns during evening. Sub Section of No 4 Section relieved Sub Section of No 2 Section during the night, relief completed correct by 11 pm. A quiet uneventful 24 hrs, except for heavy shelling with Gas Shell for a short period in the Nieuport Bains Sector. Experimented with a T. Shaped base designed in the company & found satisfactory. Pte Wilson rejoined from F.A. 2/Lt Smith & Pte Mellor rejoined from leave. Sick Nil Casualties Nil. Strength of Company 11 Officers 213 Other Ranks.	[signature]
Coast Defences Nieuport Bains – St Idesbalde	23/8/14	Thurs.	A dull day, Rain during forenoon. hostile aerial activity during early hours of morning. Visited by C.M.G.O during afternoon. Several Points of Interest discussed. 2 Men of No 4 Section to F.A suspected suffering from Gas poisoning. A quiet uneventful 24 hours. Sick 2. Casualties Nil. Strength of Company 11 Officers 213 Other Ranks.	[signature]
Coast Defences Nieuport Bains – St Idesbalde	24/8/14	Fri	A fine day, very windy during forenoon. Lt Hanagan to leave to U.K. O C Coy reconnoitred Forward area during afternoon & back areas during the evening. Sub Section in Reserve carried out Barrage Drill & Training. Coxyde was subjected to a desultory shelling during the afternoon & evening & several fell in Coy Hd Qr area. Otherwise a quiet uneventful 24 hours. Sick Nil Casualties Nil Strength of Coy 11 officers 213 Other RKs	[signature]

2353 Wt. W2544/1454 700,000 5/15 D. D. & L. A.D.S.S./Forms/C. 2118.

Page 8.

Instructions regarding War Diaries and Intelligence Summaries are contained in F. S. Regs., Part II. and the Staff Manual respectively. Title pages will be prepared in manuscript.

WAR DIARY of 144 MACHINE GUN COMPANY
~~or~~
~~INTELLIGENCE SUMMARY.~~
(Erase heading not required.)

for AUGUST 1914

Army Form C. 2118.

Place	Date	Hour Day	Summary of Events and Information	Remarks and references to Appendices
Coast Defences Nieuport Bains – St Idesbalde	25/8/14	Sat.	A cool day very windy, inclined to Rain. About 10 am 1 heavy shell fell into the horse lines, result 1 Killed & 3 others injured (1 horse 3 Mules). Got remainder clear & moved out for a few hours. Lt Clarke to F.A Sick. Lt Phillips & Sgt Bates rejoined from G.H.Q, M.G School. Pt Taylor from F.A. to duty. A quiet night. Sick 1. Casualties Nil Strength of Coy 11 officers 213 Other Ranks.	[signature]
Coast Defences Nieuport Bains – St Idesbalde	26/8/14	Sun.	A fine day, cool. Reserve Sub Section training in Barrage Work during forenoon. Lt Phillips relieved Capt Bain in command of Right Sector during the afternoon. A quiet uneventful 24 hours in Billet area. Sick Nil, Casualties Nil. Strength of Coy 11 offrs 213 other Rks. (1 offr leave) (D. Rs 4 leave. 5 C of I. 6. Sick)	[signature]
Coast Defences Nieuport Bains – St Idesbalde	27/8/14	Mon.	A very stormy day, wind & rain throughout the day. O.C Coy visited all Posts during the day. all correct. Sub Section No 1 Sect relieved Sub Section No 4. Nieuport Bains area. Relief completed by 11 pm. A quiet uneventful 24 hours. Sick Nil, Casualties Nil, Strength of Company 11 offrs 213 other Ranks. (1 offr leave. 10 Present. 6 OR. leave. 5 Course of Instn. 6 Sick. Field Amb. 196 Present.	[signature]
Coast Defences Nieuport Bains – St Idesbalde	28/8/14	Tues.	Another stormy day, high wind & rain throughout day. 144 Inf Bde relieved & company now under orders of 199th Inf Brigade. Sub Section No 4 Section relieved Sub Section No 1 Section at St Idesbalde. Relief completed correct by 4 pm. 1 O.R. Reinforcement from Base. 1 OR to C.C.S. 1 OR from C.R.S. A quiet uneventful 24 hours. Sick Nil Casualties Nil Strength of Company 11 offrs 213 Other Ranks	[signature]
Coast Defences Nieuport Bains – St Idesbalde	29/8/14	Wed.	Another stormy day Visited by DMGO 49 Div during forenoon. 2 O.R to leave U.K. 1 OR to Course of Instn. Hostile Shelling in vicinity of Coy HQ from 9.40 pm to midnight. T. Mortar Billet 500 yards away hit & several casualties inflicted. Sub Section No 1 Section relieved Sub Section No 4 in NIEUPORT BAINS Sector. relief complete 9.30 pm.	A.S. [illegible]

2353 Wt. W2544/1454 700,000 5/15 D. D. & L. A.D.S.S./Forms/C. 2118.

PAGE 9

Instructions regarding War Diaries and Intelligence Summaries are contained in F. S. Regs., Part II. and the Staff Manual respectively. Title pages will be prepared in manuscript.

Army Form C. 2118.

WAR DIARY of 147 Machine Gun Company – or ~~INTELLIGENCE SUMMARY.~~

(*Erase heading not required.*)

for AUGUST 1917 –

Place	~~Date~~	DAY ~~Hour~~	Summary of Events and Information	Remarks and references to Appendices
Coast Defences NIEUPORT BAINS – St. IDESBALDE	30/8/17	Thurs.	A Stormy day – Capt. J. Inchley MC & 2 OR left for MG Course CAMIERS – Lieut A B Sillman assumed temporarily Command of Company. Capt C.W.C. Bain 2nd in Command – Strength of Company 11 officers 213 O.R. 9 officers present 1 leave 1 course OR. 198 present 8 leave 4 courses 3 sick –	[illegible]

WAR DIARY

147th MACHINE GUN COMPANY - OPERATION ORDERS No 1.
OOST DUNKIRK. 13.8.17.
REFERENCE MAP OOST DUNKIRK. SHEET 11. 1/40000.

****

1. The 147th Machine Gun Company will relieve the 148th M.G.Coy in the Coast Defences (Forward area) on the 14/8/17.

2. DISPOSITIONS.
No 1 Section will relieve "A" Section of 148th Company on RIGHT.
No 2 Section will relieve "B" Section 148th Company on RIGHT CENTRE.
No 3 Section will relieve "C" Section 148th Company on LEFT CENTRE.
Sub-Section No 4 Section will relieve "D" Sub Section 148th Company on LEFT.
Company Headquarters , Transport, one Sub Section No 4 Section will move to, and remain at COXYDE BAINS.

3. GUIDES.
Guides for Sections will be met as follows:-

For RIGHT Section For RIGHT CENTRE Section.	At Cross Roads OOST DUNKIRK (R.27.c.19.70.) at 2am.BAINS
For LEFT CENTRE SECTION. For LEFT SUB SECTION.	At Cross Roads COXYDE BAINS. (X.6.a.95.65.) at 3.0am.

4. AMMUNITION, STORES, etc.,
Reserve ammunition, trench stores, reports etc., also 14 belt boxes per gun will be taken over on relief, and a list of all stores etc., sent in to Company Headquarters with relief reports. Sections will hand in to Q.M.Stores before leaving OOST DUNKIRK belt boxes as follows.

No 1 Section	56	Boxes.
No 2 Section	56	"
No 3 Section	56	"
No 4 Section	28	"

Section Mobile Reserve S.A.A will not accompany Sections.

5. COMMANDS.
Sections will be commanded in line by the following:-
No 1 Section 2/Lieut W.J.SLATER.
No 2 Section Lieut P.A.HANAGHAN.
No 3 Section Lieut H,S.BOXER.
S,S,No 4 Section 2/Lieut W.S.COATES.

6 DRESS.
Dress for movement Marching Order. Valises will be taken into line (carried on limbers.)

7. RATIONS.
Rations 14th instant taken into line with sections.
For 15th and onwards further instructions will be issued.,

8. REPORTS.
A Cycle Orderly will accompany each Section, he will receive relief reports and handing over lists and proceed with same to Company Headquarters COXYDE BAINS.

9. TRANSPORT.
Fighting limbers only will accompany Sections, proceeding direct to Transport Lines COXYDE BAINS after completion of duty.

10. MOVES.
Company Headquarters will close at OOST DUNKIRK at 9.0am, and re-open at COXYDE BAINS at 9.0am 14th inst.

[signature] Captain.

Comndg 147th Machine Gun Company.

SECRET.

147th MACHINE GUN COMPANY * OPERATION ORDERS. No 2 .

COMYDE BAINS - 19.8.17. - Reference Map Sheet 11. 1/40000.

1. Inter-Section reliefs will be carried out on the dates specified as follows:

2. One Sub-Section No 1 Section willbe relieved by Reserve Sub-Section No 4 Section on the night of 20th/21st instant.
A Sub-Section No 1 Section will on relief return to COMYDE BAINS becoming Sub-Section in Reserve.

3. One Sub-Section of No 4 Section will be relieved by Reserve Sub-Section No 1 Section on the night of 21st/22nd instant.
Sub-Section No 4 Section will on relief return to Company Headquarters COMYDE BAINS, becoming Reserve Sub-Section.

4. One Sub-Section No 1 Section in the RIGHT SECTOR will be relieve by Reserve Sub-Section No 4 Section on the night 22nd/23rd instant.
Sub-Section of No 1 Section will on relief return to Company Headquarters COMYDE BAINS, becoming Sub-Section in Reserve.

5. OFFICERS RELIEFS.
Lieut W.J.[illegible] will relieve Lieut P.A.HANAGHAN on morning 20th inst. Command of the RIGHT CENTRE SECTOR will pass to Lieut W.J.[illegible] at 10.0am 20th instant.

Capt C/W.G.BAIN will relieve 2/Lieut W.J.LEAMER on night 20th/21st ins Command of RIGHT SECTOR will pass to Capt C/W.G.BAIN at 11pm 20thinst

2/Lieut W.J.LEAMER will on return to Company Headquarters assume command of Reserve Sub-Section.

[illegible].8.17.

Captain.
Comdg 147th Machine Gun Company.

S E C R E T

147th MACHINE GUN COMPANY - OPERATION ORDERS No 3.

Headquarters - COXYDE BAINS - 26.8.17. Reference Map Sheet 11 1/40000

1. INTER SECTION RELIEFS will be carried out on the dates specified as follows.

2. One Sub-Section No 4 Section will be relieved by Reserve Sub Sectn No 1 Section on the night 27th/28th instant. Sub Section No 4 Sectn on relief will return to COXYDE BAINS becoming Sub Section in Reserve

3. One Sub Section of No 1 Section will be relieved by Reserve Sub-Section No 4 Section on the night 28th.29th instant. Sub Section No 1 Section on relief will return to Company Headquarters COXYDE BAINS, becoming Sub Section in Reserve.

4. One Sub-Section No 4 Section will be relieved by Sub Section No 1 Section on the night 29th/30th instant. Sub Section No 4 Section on relief will return to Company Headquarters COXYDE BAINS becoming Sub Section in Reserve.

5. OFFICERS RELIEFS.
Lieut J.S.PHILLIPS will relieve Capt G.W.C.BAIN on forenoon 26th instant. Command of the RIGHT SECTOR will pass to Lieut J.S.PHILLIPS at 3.0pm 26th instant.
2/Lieut W.J.SLATER will relieve Lieut H.S.BOYER on the forenoon 27th instant. Command of LEFT CENTRE SECTOR will pass to 2/Lieut SLATER at 12 Noon 27th instant.
Lieut J.S.PHILLIPS will relieve Lieut W.J.[illegible] on forenoon 30th instant. Command of the RIGHT CENTRE SECTOR will pass to Lieut J.S.PHILLIPS at Noon 30th instant.
2/Lieut H.SMITH will relieve Lieut J.S PHILLIPS on the night of 29th/30th instant. Command of the RIGHT SECTOR will pass to 2/Lieut H.SMITH at 11.0pm 29th instant.

26.8.17. Copy No 4 Captain.
Comndg 147th Machine Gun Company.

Copies
No 1 To O.C. No 1 Section.
No 2 To O.C. No 2 Section.
No 3 To O.C. No 3 Section.
No 4 To O.C. No 4 Section.
No 5 To Company Headquarters.
No 6 & 7 WAR DIARY.

Secret

War Diary Vol 21

of

144 Machine Gun Coy

for

September 1917

Confidential

War Diary of

147th Machine Gun Coy

dated

1/9/17 to 30/9/17

PAGE 1

Army Form C. 2118.

Instructions regarding War Diaries and Intelligence Summaries are contained in F. S. Regs., Part II. and the Staff Manual respectively. Title pages will be prepared in manuscript.

WAR DIARY or ~~INTELLIGENCE SUMMARY.~~ of 147th MACHINE GUN COMPANY for SEPTEMBER 1917.

(Erase heading not required.)

Place	Date	~~Hour~~	Summary of Events and Information	Remarks and references to Appendices
COAST defences NIEUPORT BAINS – St IDESBALDE	31/8/17	Fri:	Finer weather – OC Coy was sent for in morning by Brigadier 199 Bgd: with reference to taking two MG's from COXYDE BAINS & placing them at LA PANNE. Went to LA PANNE to make arrangements with OC 2/7 Manchesters by whom one half section are to be rationed etc: Lt Hall & 2 Lt Coates went to lecture on "barrage fire" in afternoon at BRAY DUNES by Major Barry MC. There seems to be an epidemic in the Company of stomach chills both among officers & other ranks, possibly due to sudden change in weather conditions – Strength of Coy 11 off 212 OR.	AmB
	1/9/17	Sat.	Officers on strength of Coy. Capt. T. Mumbly MC Comng: (on CAMIERS Course) Lieut. G B Silleman 2 i/c (acting OC.) Capt. C W C Bain OC No 4 Secn (acting 2 i/c) Lieut Boxer Comm No 3 Secn Lieut Hall Comm No 2 Secn: 2 Lt Smith Comm No 1 Secn. Lt. Hanaghan (on leave) Sub secn officer No 2 Secn. Lt. Phillips sub secn off No 4 Secn 2 Lt Slater Sub secn off No 1 Secn 2 Lt Coates sub secn off No 3 Lt Foulds Transport officer CSM Mitchell CQMS Sykes – Distribution of Coy on 1st Sept as follows: Coy HQ COXYDE BAINS also half section No 4. Remainder of Coy on Coast Defence as follows:– No 1. NIEUPORT BAINS No 2 OOST DUNKIRK BAINS No 3. COXYDE BAINS. No 4 Half section at ST IDESBALDE Strength of Coy: 11 off: 212 OR. CSM Mitchell on Course of physical training, his place taken by Sgt Hopper No 2 Secn – Sgt Ward (No 1 Secn) returned from months "time expired" leave – Weather prevented any out of door training by sub section at Coy HQ. Rain & gale of wind all day, also very cold. Enemy shelled Coxyde BAINS during afternoon	AmB
	2/9/17	Sun.	Very stormy day – Draft of one riding horse arrived, poor animal, it was shot by Vet officer after Transport Officer had ridden it to LA PANNE. Sub-secn of No 4 training in morning. Enemy shelled COXYDE BAINS during afternoon – Sub-secn of No 3 under Lt Boxer moved from COXYDE BAINS to fresh Coast Defence positions at LA PANNE, rationed by 3/4 Manchesters. Left Coy HQ 5.30pm reported in position 8.50 pm. One man FA. Strength of Coy 11 off: 211. OR.	AmB

2353 Wt. W2544/1454 700,000 5/15 D. D. & L. A.D.S.S./Forms/C. 2118.

PAGE 2.

Instructions regarding War Diaries and Intelligence Summaries are contained in F. S. Regs., Part II. and the Staff Manual respectively. Title pages will be prepared in manuscript.

WAR DIARY of 147th MACHINE GUN COMPANY

~~INTELLIGENCE SUMMARY.~~ for SEPTEMBER 1917 -

(Erase heading not required.)

Army Form C. 2118.

Place	Date	~~Hour~~ day -	Summary of Events and Information	Remarks and references to Appendices
Coast Defences NIEUPORT BAINS to ST IDESBALDE	3/9/17	Mon:	Much finer day - gale having subsided - No 4 Section relieved No 1 Section in Right Positions - Sub secn of No 4 at C.H.Q. leaving at 9 am - One Subsection of No 1 to Coy HQ the other Subsecn: to ST IDESBALDE - under 2 Lt Slater - 2 Lt Smith at Coy HQ. Lt Phillips in Command of No 4 section in Right positions relief complete 3.30 pm. 1 man FASEK. 11 off 211 or	A.B.
"	4/9/17	Tues.	Fine day - Company paid out - Visit from Col: Clarke CMGO. 3pm - 4pm who reported that he had been round all our positions, he was very pleased with everything, except that the cleanliness on RIGHT positions was not quite up to the mark. Indented for large quantity of RE Stores for improving accomodation at RIGHT & CENTRE positions. Strength of Coy. 11 off 211 or Capt. Bain to ROSENDALE re laundry arrangements -	A.B.
"	5/9/17	Wed:	Lieut Foulds to 147 Bgd & ASC re obtaining new mount & other matters - LC Pinder returned from Transport Course Between 8.30 pm & 10 pm hostile planes dropped several bombs in neighbourhood of COXYDE BAINS, two dropping about 300 yards from Coy HQ, in Heavy Artillery camp, ~~wounding~~ killing one man & wounding two - One man of 147 MGC slightly cut on face by small piece of bomb or fuse from A.A. shell, remained on duty - As the Artillery had no RAMC man or stretcher we gave assistance. Pt Wilkinson (att from RAMC) kept up his reputation by rendering prompt & valuable aid - Strength of Coy: 11 officers, 211 or	A.B.
"	6/9/17	Thurs:	Fine day. Lt Hanaghan returned from leave - About 50 5.9 shells were dropped around Nos 7 & 8 gun positions between 10-11.30 pm - No damage done. All sections working with a view to improving winter quaters Strength of Coy. 11 off. 212 oR.	A.B.

2353 Wt. W2544/1454 700,000 5/15 D. D. & L. A.D.S.S./Forms/C. 2118.

PAGE 3

Instructions regarding War Diaries and Intelligence Summaries are contained in F. S. Regs., Part II. and the Staff Manual respectively. Title pages will be prepared in manuscript.

WAR DIARY of 147th MACHINE GUN COMPANY or ~~INTELLIGENCE SUMMARY.~~ for SEPTEMBER 1917.

(*Erase heading not required.*)

Army Form C. 2118.

Place	Date	~~Hour~~ Day.	Summary of Events and Information	Remarks and references to Appendices
Coast Defences NIEUPORT BAINS to LA PANNE	7/9/17	Fri	This day Corps M.G.O visited Right positions at 7am, expressed himself very satisfied, especially with one gun about which he was very complimentary. Lieut Sellman (Temp OC Coy) left at 3pm to attend course of instruction with Div RFA. in "Barrage work" until 9th inst. Capt Bain assumed command of Coy. Lieut Foulds (T.O) went out on his race horse & returned with a badly strained side. Lieut Hall represented the company at a meeting to decide details of a Brigade Boxing Championship. We are going to enter as strongly as possible, & will arrange preliminary bouts, training etc. The DMGO 66th Divn round, wants R2 AA position moving, as apparently it is annoying RGA people in the vicinity. We decide to see Brigade about it. Strength of Coy 11 offs 212 or.	CEB
	8/9/17	Sat.	A dull day. Lt Foulds in bed suffering from strain. OC Coy visited Lt. Phillips in Right Sector & found all correct. On return found note from Lt. Boxer to say that Pt Woodhead No 3 Section had shot himself through the hand. Enquiries are being made. Remainder of day normal. Casualties 1 self-inflicted. Strength of Coy 11 off. 211 or.	CEB
	9/9/17	Sun.	No 1 Section relieved No 4 Section in RIGHT Sector. Capt Bain to LA PANNE in morning to see No 3 Section. Found all correct. Sections employed in making winter shelters. Lieut Sellman returned & he assumed command of Company. A fair day. Strength of Coy. 11 offs. 211 or.	CEB

PAGE . 4

Instructions regarding War Diaries and Intelligence Summaries are contained in F. S. Regs., Part II. and the Staff Manual respectively. Title pages will be prepared in manuscript.

WAR DIARY ~~or~~ of 147th MACHINE GUN COMPANY ~~INTELLIGENCE SUMMARY.~~ for SEPTEMBER 1917 -

(Erase heading not required.)

Army Form C. 2118.

Place	Date	~~Hour~~ Day	Summary of Events and Information	Remarks and references to Appendices
Coast Defences NIEUPORT BAINS to LA PANNE	10/9/17	Mon -	Fine day - Sections in line continued to improve positions - Lieut Hall training the men entered for Divisional boxing Championship - Enemy artillery unusually active in NIEUPORT Sector - Strength of Coy 11 offs 212 or.	A.W.S.
	11/9/17	Tues -	Fine day One winter shelter completed at RIGHT positions, another started - Work continued on Shelter at OOST DUNKIRK positions - a good deal of hostile shelling about 500 yds South of OOST DUNKIRK BAINS during evening - O.C. Coy visited 147 Bgd HQ in afternoon. Strength of Coy 11 offs. 212 OR	A.W.S.
	12/9/17	Wed.	Fine day. Lieut Phillips leave to U.K. Cookhouse completed at Right-Centre position. Emplacements worked upon at COXYDE positions. Right positions improved & further work done on winter shelters. Work done on shelters at ST IDESBALDE positions. OC Coy visited 147 Inf Bgd during afternoon - Heard that 4 & 5 R.W.W. move to BRAY DUNES tomorrow Thursday. Strength of Coy 11 offs. 212 or.	A.W.S.
	13/9/17	Thrs.	Enemy shelled COXYDE BAINS during early hours of morning - Right Centre positions freely shelled by H.V. guns 11 to 11 45 pm (12) 1.30 - 4.30 am (13th) Latrine rebuilt at Right Centre positions - Winter shelter for Right position completed. Strength of Coy 11 offs 212 or - Boxing competitors to 147 Bgd in evening to "weigh in" - OC Coy visited 147 Bgd -	A.W.S.
	14/9/17	Friday -	Fine day but cold - Right Section (No 1) heavily shelled between 6 & 9 pm - One man wounded in hand - Pt BRADLEY - Lieut ~~Sirlatt~~ reports that Pt Field & Pt Duckett did good work in attending the wounded of the RFA who were hit at the same time, notwithstanding the shelling - Work continued on improving winter shelters etc. Strength of Coy 11 offs 211 or -	A.W.S.

2353 Wt. W2544/1454 700,000 5/15 D. D. & L. A.D.S.S./Forms/C. 2118.

PAGE 5

Instructions regarding War Diaries and Intelligence Summaries are contained in F. S. Regs., Part II. and the Staff Manual respectively. Title pages will be prepared in manuscript.

Army Form C. 2118.

WAR DIARY of 147th MACHINE GUN COMPANY.

~~INTELLIGENCE SUMMARY.~~

(*Erase heading not required.*)

for SEPTEMBER - 1917 -

Place	Date	~~Hour~~ DAY	Summary of Events and Information	Remarks and references to Appendices
Coast Defences NIEUPORT BAINS to LA PANNE	15/9/17	Sat.	A fine day - No 4 Section under Lieut Hanaghan relieved No 1 Section in the Right Sector. Lieut Hanaghan assumed command of No 4 Section in the absence of Lt Phillips on leave - Lieut Stillman & 2 Lieut Coates went to gas lecture at GHYVELDE. Work done on winter positions. Heard that Coy was to be relieved on 17th by 146 MGC. (warning note only) Strength of Coy: 11 offs 211 or. -	AnS
COAST DEFENCES NIEUPORT BAINS to LA PANNE	16/9/17	Sun:	Fine day - Preparing for relief by 146 MGC. Their 2 in Command came over, & they promise to leave GHYVELDE at 7 am & to take over our belt boxes in the line, i.e. 14 per gun - OC Coy went to 147 Bgd LA PANNE in evening, to arrange for leaving men to stay with Brigade when we move. Strength of Coy 11 offs. 210 or. -	AnS
GHYVELDE	17/9/17	Mon. -	Company relieved in Coast Defence positions by 146 MG Coy. Relief reported complete by 5.20 pm - Company went to billets at 49 Divn: rest camp at GHYVELDE (under canvas) (transport at [illegible] Farm) - No 4 Section arrived at billets late owing to heavy shelling at NIEUPORT BAINS, which held up relief; they arrived at 8.30 pm - Relieving officer in right sector was killed by a shell, which also shook Lieut Hanaghan up considerably, but he was able to follow on later, having got a lift in an ambulance - The 146 MGC. did not take over belt boxes after all as arranged - Coy S. Major returned from course at ST POL. Coy Strength 11 offs 211 or	AnS
GHYVELDE	18/9/17	Tues	A wet, dull day - Company spent morning cleaning up gun equipment etc - Capt Bain rode over to a Brigade Conference, to discuss plans for a Brigade practice attack - Coy S. Major for months leave - Sgt Pearson left the Company to become Instructor at Grantham - Strength of Coy 11 offs 209 or. -	AnS

2353 Wt. W2544/1454 700,000 5/15 D. D. & L. A.D.S.S./Forms/C. 2118.

PAGE 6 -

Instructions regarding War Diaries and Intelligence Summaries are contained in F. S. Regs., Part II. and the Staff Manual respectively. Title pages will be prepared in manuscript.

WAR DIARY or ~~INTELLIGENCE SUMMARY.~~ of 147th MACHINE GUN COMPANY for SEPTEMBER 1917.

(Erase heading not required.)

Army Form C. 2118.

Place	Date	~~Hour~~ Day	Summary of Events and Information	Remarks and references to Appendices
GHYVELDE	19/9/17	Wed.	A fine day. Nos 3+4 Sections took part in a practice Brigade attack at BRAY DUNES. Nos 1+2 Secns "barrage" drill in morning – Heard at 4.20 pm that Brigade Boxing Championship would come off at LA PANNE at 5 pm. OC Coy managed to borrow a car from an R E Coy + took competitors + 6 others over, arrived 5.20 pm – The MGC won the middles (Pt Readman) Feathers (Pt Riley) + runner up in "welters" (Pt Snowball) The Coy had more entries than any other unit + was congratulated by GOC. In "Times" of 17th inst. Lieut Hall gains the Military Cross – Strength of Coy. 11 off. 209 OR.	AwS.
	20/9/17	Thrs.	Heavy rain during night. Lieut Foulds leave to U.K. Sections training in morning on "barrage" drill PT in afternoon. Heard that we were to move on 23 inst. OC Coy + Capt Bain to 147 Inf: Bgd. in Evening re a "barrage" which Division had ordered us to do, but it was decided that we had not had enough practice to do a demonstration, + we should simply do drill + firing on the Sands – Strength of Coy. 11 off + 209 or.	AwS.
	21/9/17	Fri.	Lieut. Hanaghan left for Corps Rest Camp with slight Shell Shock – Company left billets at 9.30 am taking with them haversack rations for "barrage" work on Dunes – Returned to Camp at 5.15 pm – Very successful day, Capt Bain went to Bgd. LA PANNE to arrange billeting – Very fine day – Strength of Coy. 11 off 209 or – Orders came that the Brigade are to move on 23rd inst to TETEGHEM.	AwS

2353 Wt. W2544/1454 700,000 5/15 D. D. & L. A.D.S.S./Forms/C. 2118.

PAGE 7.

Instructions regarding War Diaries and Intelligence Summaries are contained in F. S. Regs., Part II. and the Staff Manual respectively. Title pages will be prepared in manuscript.

Army Form C. 2118.

WAR DIARY ~~or~~ of 147th MACHINE GUN Coy: ~~INTELLIGENCE SUMMARY.~~ for September 1917.

(Erase heading not required.)

Place	Date	Day	Summary of Events and Information	Remarks and references to Appendices
GHYVELDE	22/9/17	Sat.	Fine day. Company started morning cleaning up preparatory to moving on following day. At 11.30 am orders came for Coy. to go down to beach for barrage work. Sections returned at 3.30 pm - Rest of day Coy very busy packing & cleaning up. Strength 11 off 209 or.	[initials]
TETEGHEM.	23/9/17	Sun.	Lieut Silliman went to CAMIERS to attend a demonstration in MG barrage - 12 noon Coy left GHYVELDE for TETEGHEM. En route Coy marched past Divisional General. He expressed himself pleased with the marching & said the turn out of the transport was very good, the metal work being excellent. Arrived in billets near ROSENDAEL at 5 pm most of the men very fit a few bad feet. Strength of Coy 11 off 209 or.	[initials]
	24/9/17	Mon	Coy left billets 9.45 am arrived WORMHOUDT 3.20 pm a 15 mile march on bad roads - men tired out at finish but marching throughout excellent. Foot inspection immediately on arrival, feet in bad condition. Strength 11 off - 209 or -	[initials]
BUYSSCHEURE	25/9/17	Tues	Coy left WORMHOUDT area 7.15 am & marched to BUYSSCHEURE 12 miles - The men with worst feet were put on a lorry & remainder marched through without a man falling out, a good record considering state of feet. Arrived in billets at 11.30 am - found lunch ready. Remainder of day spent in foot inspections etc. Strength of coy 11 off 209 or -	[initials]

2353 Wt. W2544/1454 700,000 5/15 D. D. & L. A.D.S.S./Forms/C. 2118.

PAGE 8

Instructions regarding War Diaries and Intelligence Summaries are contained in F. S. Regs., Part II. and the Staff Manual respectively. Title pages will be prepared in manuscript.

Army Form C. 2118.

WAR DIARY ~~or~~ of 147th MACHINE GUN COMPANY
INTELLIGENCE ~~SUMMARY~~. for SEPTEMBER 1917

(*Erase heading not required.*)

Place	Date	~~Hour~~ DAY	Summary of Events and Information	Remarks and references to Appendices
BUYSSCHEERE	26/9/17	Wed	A very hot day. Barrage drill in morning – Lieut Sellman returned from CAMIERS in afternoon – Strength of Coy 11 off 209 or –	ABS.
	27/9/17	Thrs	A very hot day. Heavy sick parade 21 men – Busy preparing for move – Strength of Coy 11 off 209 or	ABS.
WESTBECOURT	28/9/17	Fri.	Company moved to WESTBECOURT marching through St MOMELIN – ST OMER & QUELMES. a 33 Kilos – march. Left at 8.45 am, arrived in billets 6 pm. A two hour halt for lunch 12.50 – 2.50 – men marched very well not a man falling out – Strength of Coy 11 off 209 or –	ABS.
ESQUERDES	29/9/17	Sat	Fine day – 2 Lt Coates + 10 or left for leave UK. Morning begun cleaning up – Received sudden orders from Bgd, to move to ESQUERDES as soon as possible. Moved off 3.30 pm – arrived at ESQUERDES 6 pm – Capt. Mulhig returned from CAMIERS & resumed Command of Coy. Strength of Coy. 11 off 206 or –	ABS.
STAPLES	30/9/17	Sun.	A fine day – Coy left ESQUERDES 8.15 am for STAPLES via ARQUES, FORT ROUGE & LENIEPPE distance about 23 Kilos – Men again marched well, no man falling out – A 2 hour halt noon to 2 pm for dinner – Strength of Coy. 11 off – 206 or –	ABS.

A. B. Sellman Lieut –
acting OC 147 Machine Gun Company –
30th Sept 1917 –

2353 Wt. W2544/1454 700,000 5/15 D. D. & L. A.D.S.S./Forms/C. 2118.

147th Machine Gun Company OPERATION ORDERS No 8.
HEADQUARTERS GHYVELDE Dated 22.9.17.

---

1. The 147th Machine Gun Company will move to TETEGHEM tomorrow the 23th instant.

2. ROUTE :- PONT DE GHYVELDE - PONT DE ZUYDCOOTE - LEFFRINCKOUKE - TETEGHEM.

3. Company will parade ready to move off at 12 Noon.

4. DRESS :- Marching Order.

5. Dinner for Company will be at 11.0am.

6. Section Commanders will see that their tents are left in a scrupulously clean condition.

7. One limber will call for Officers valises at 10.0am to take them to Transport lines where they will be packed in Section limbers.

8. One limber for Orderly Room and Cook's stores will be at the Orderly Room at 11.15am.

9 Transport will be at GHYVELDE CHURCH at 12 Noon ready to follow the Company.

10. 200 yards distance will be maintained between the Company and the Transport on the march.

11. ACKNOWLEDGE RECEIPT.

22.9.17.

(Sd) C.W.C.BAIN. Captain.
2-in-C 147th Machine Gun Company.

Copy 9

SECRET.
****

147th MACHINE GUN COMPANY * OPERATION ORDERS No 7.
HEADQUARTERS - COXYDE BAINS - Dated 16.9.17. Reference Map Sheet 11.
1/40000.

1. The 147th Machine Gun Company will be relieved ~~by~~ in the Coast Defence Positions by the 146th Machine Gun Company on the 17th instant.

2. Sections on their relief will proceed independently to GHYVELDE where they will be met at the Church by Guides.

3. Guides from No 2 Section and Sub Section of No 3 at COXYDE will report at Company Headquarters at 10.30am.
Guide from No 3 Section at LA PANNE will be at the Horse Standings LA PANNE Square at 9.30am.
Guide from No 1 Section will be at the DUNES HOTEL ST IDESBALDE at 10.0am.
A Runner from Headquarters will act as Guide for RIGHT SECTOR, and will report at Company Headquarters at 11.0am.
Lieut HANAGHAN will arrange Guides to meet Section of 146th Machine Gun Company at OOST DUNKIRK BAINS at 11.0am.
A Cyclist will be at LA PANNE Cross Roads at 9.30am to direct relieving Unit.

4. Details of "Work in progress" will be handed over.

5. All "T" shaped bases in possession of sections will be taken to GHYVELDE.

6. Trench Stores will be handed over, handing over lists to be rendered to Company Headquarters in duplicate.

7. Captain BAIN and three Other Ranks will proceed to GHYVELDE as billeting party on the morning of the 17th instant.

8. 14 belt boxes per gun will be handed over to the 146th Machine Gun Company. 196 boxes to replace these will be taken over by the 147th Machine Gun Company at GHYVELDE.

9. All billets will be left scrupulously clean.

10 Sections will make their own arrangements as to dinners.

11. Relief complete to be reported to Company Headquarters COXYDE BAINS.

12. ACKNOWLEDGE RECEIPT.

16.9.17.

A.B. Sellman Lieut

Comndg 147th Machine Gun Company.

Copy No 1 to O.C. No 4 Section.
Copy No 2 to O.C. No 2 Section.
Copy No 3 to O.C. No 3 Section.
Copy No 4 to ~~[illegible]~~ 2/Lt COATES.
Copy No 5 to O.C. No 1 Section.
Copy No 6 to Lieut FOULDS.
Copy No 7 to 147th I.B.
Copy No 8 & 9 War Diary.
Copy No 10 Office.
" " 11. 146 M.G.C.

147th MACHINE GUN COMPANY OPERATION ORDERS NO 10.
HEADQUARTERS WORMHOULT Dated 24.9.17. for 25.9.17.

---

1. The Company will move to BROXEELE tomorrow morning the 25th instant.

2 REVEILLE 5.0am. BREAKFAST 5.30am.

3. <u>Parades</u>
Company parade on road by Transport billet, facing EAST, ready to move off at 7.15am.

4. Order of Sections 1,3,4 & 2.

5. Billets to be left in a clean condition.

6. Mess Cart to be at Officers Mess at 6.30am.

7. Men detailed by Section Commanders to ride in the lorry will report at H.Q.Farm at 7.0am.

24.9.17.

(Sd) C.W.C.BAIN. Captain.
Commdg. 147th Machine Gun Company.

147th MACHINE GUN COMPANY OPERATION ORDER No 9.
HEADQUARTERS TETEGHEM. Dated 23.9.17. for 24.9.17.

1. REVEILLE 6.30am BREAKFAST 7.0am.

2. Limbers to be packed by 8.30am.

3. Section Officers will detail any men unfit to march to be at TETEGHEM CHURCH at 6.45am, having at Breakfast. They will report to O.C. MOTOR AMBULANCE.

4. Billets to be evacuated, clean and tidy.

5. Headquarters limber, and Mess Cart to be at Headquarters at 8.0am.

6. Orders as to time and place of Company parade will be issued later.

23.9.17. (Sd) C.W.C.BAIN. Captain.

Comndg 147th Machine Gun Company.

Copies to O.C. No 1,2,3 & 4 Sections.
Transport H.Q, and 2 for Diary.

147th MACHINE GUN COMPANY * OPERATION ORDERS No 9.
HEADQUARTERS TETEGHEM Dated 23.9.17. for 24.9.17.

1. REVEILLE 6.30am. BREAKFAST 7.0am.

2. Limbers to be packed by 8.30am.

3. Section Officers will detail any men unfit to march to be at TETEGHEM CHURCH at 6.45am, having had breakfast. They will report to O.C. MOTOR AMBULANCE.

4. Billets to be evacuated clean and tidy.

5. Headquarter limber and Mess Cart to be at Headquarters at 8.0am.

6. Orders as to time and place of Company parade will be issued later.

23.9.17. (Sd) C.W.C.BAIN. Captain.

Comndg 147th Machine Gun Company.

Copies to Nos 1,2,3 & 4 Sections.
Transport. H.Q. and 2 for diary.

S E C R E T.

147th MACHINE GUN COMPANY * OPERATION ORDERS No 6.

1. No 4 Section will relieve No 1 Section in the RIGHT SECTOR tomorrow the 15th instant.
   One Sub Section No 4 Section will leave Company Headquarters at 9.30am.
   Sub Section of No 4 Section willleave ST IDESBALDE on relief be/ Sub Section No 1 Section.
2. Lieut HANAGHAN will assume Command temporarily of No 4 Section and from Noon on 15th instant will be in Command of the RIGHT SECTOR.
3. ACKNOWLEDGE RECEIPT.
4. Relief complete to be reported to Company Headquarters.

No 1 Copy to O.C. No 1 Section.
No 2 Copy to 2/Lieut SLATER.
No 3 Copy to Lieut HANAGHAN.
No 4 Copy to OFFICE.
No 5 & 6 Copies to WAR DIARY.

14.9.17. A.B. Sellman Lieut

Comdg 147th Machine Gun Company.

147th MACHINE GUN COMPANY * OPERATION ORDER No 4 S E C R E T.
HEADQUARTERS - COXYDE BAINS - 2.9.17. Ref Map Sheet 11 1/40000

1. Inter Section reliefs and alteration in dispositions will be carried out as follows:

2. One Sub Section of No 3 Section under Lieut H.H.TODD will move from COXYDE BAINS to LA PANNE at 6.30pm on SUNDAY the 2nd inst, to occupy Coast Defence Positions. They will be rationed from and after that date by the 2/7th Lancashires.

3. No 1 Section will be relieved in RIGHT SECTOR on Monday 3rd instant by No 4 Section. The one Sub Section of No 4 now at Company H.Qrs will relieve the one sub Section of No 1 in the morning who will go direct to ST IDESBALDE. The Sub Section of No 4 now at ST IDESBALDE will relieve the one sub Section of No 1 on their relief.

4. One officer from No 1 Section will assume command of Sub Section No 1 at ST IDESBALDE.
2/Lieut COATES will assume command of Sub Section of No 3 at COXYDE BAINS.
Command of LEFT SECTOR will pass to Lieut [illegible] at 6.0pm 2nd inst.
Command of RIGHT SECTOR will pass to Lieut PHILLIPS at Noon on the 3rd instant.

5. ACKNOWLEDGE.

Copies. No 1

Copy No 1 to O.C. No 1 Section.
No 2 to O.C. No 3 Section.
No 3 to O.C. No 4 Section.
No 4 to 2/Lieut COATES.
No 5 to Office.
No 6 & 7 to WAR DIARY.

2.9.17.

A.B. Sillman Lieut

Comdg 147th Machine Gun Company.

Vol 22

SECRET.

WAR DIARY.

OF

1st Mach Gun Coy

FOR

1 to [illegible] October 1917

Serial Page No 9.

Instructions regarding War Diaries and Intelligence Summaries are contained in F. S. Regs., Part II. and the Staff Manual respectively. Title pages will be prepared in manuscript.

WAR DIARY or ~~INTELLIGENCE SUMMARY.~~ of 1[4?]th MACHINE GUN COMPANY for OCTOBER 1914

(Erase heading not required.)

Army Form C. 2118.

Place	Date	~~Hour~~ Day	Summary of Events and Information	Remarks and references to Appendices
STAPLES	1/10/14	Mon	Officers on strength of Coy on 1st of October 1914 Capt. J. MUNNE [?] M.C. Commdg Coy Lieut A.B Sellman 2nd in Commdg 2/Lt H Smith —"— No 1 Section 2/Lt. J.S. SLATER Sub Section Offr No 1 Section Lieut W.J. HALL M.C. —"— —"— 2 —"— Lieut J.W. BOXER Commdg No 3 Section Capt CWC BAIN Commdg No 4 Section Lieut A.C. FOULDS Transport Officer Lt. P.A. HANAGHAN Corps Rest Station Lieut J.S. PHILLIPS Cas Clearing St. 2/Lt. W.S. COATES leave to U.K. A quiet uneventful day. Sick Nil. Casualties Nil. Strength of Coy 11 offrs 206. O.R.	[illegible]
STAPLE	2/10/14	Tues	A fine day. Company carried out Training throughout the day. Barrage Work. Sick Nil. Casualties Nil. Strength of Coy 11 offrs 206 other Ranks	[illegible]
ABEELE	3/10/14	Wed	A fine day. Company moved to FORTH CAMP near ABEELE. O.C. Coy Reconnoitred forward area as far as WIELTJE VILLAGE. Sick Nil. Casualties Nil. Strength of Company 11 offrs 205 other Ranks.	[illegible]
Nr VLAMERTINGHE	4/10/14	Thurs	Company moved to YORK CAMP on the POPERINGE - YPRES ROAD, Part of Brigade in Corps Reserve. Sick Nil. Casualties nil - Strength of Coy - 11 off 205 OR -	[illegible] Lt.
ditto	5/10/14	Friday	A showery day - Company "standing by" all day ready to move up the line - Eventually the Company (less Transport + part of HQ) moved into the line to relieve N.Z. M. G. Coy - leaving YORK CAMP - ~~6.30~~ 5 pm - arriving SPREE FARM 11.30 pm. Strength of Coy 11 off 203 OR. Roads in a very bad condition -	[illegible] Lt.

Page No 10

Instructions regarding War Diaries and Intelligence Summaries are contained in F. S. Regs., Part II. and the Staff Manual respectively. Title pages will be prepared in manuscript.

WAR DIARY
or
~~INTELLIGENCE SUMMARY~~.
(Erase heading not required.)

of 147 MACHINE GUN Coy –
for October – 1917 –

Army Form C. 2118.

Place	Date	~~Hour~~ Day	Summary of Events and Information	Remarks and references to Appendices
Nr VLAMATINGE	5/10/17 Cont.	Fri.	The Coy moved into the area captured & consolidated by the 2nd Anzac Corps on 4th inst. relieving 1st & 4th NZ. Bgd. M. G. Coys – in front area from TYNE COTTAGE on the Right to KRON PRINC FARM on the Left – The relief was completed by 5.45 am 6th – A dark night & ground in an awful state, all areas being obliterated – S.O.S. sent up 3 times during night – Order of Sections No 1 on Right, & nos 2. 3 & 4 in Succession. A very rough night, but enemy rather quiet except for a desultory shelling of all areas. Transport remained for time being at YORK CAMP –	ABS
ZONNEBEKE SECTOR	6/10/17	Sat.	A Cold Showery day – Company had 8 Casualties through Shell fire – 4 Killed & 4 wounded – All no 3 Sect. The Company held on to captured area, getting good targets of enemy, who had evidently not appreciated the situation – All ranks in good Spirits – Casualties 4 Killed 1 died of wounds – 3 wounded –	ABS
"	7/10/17	Sun.	A wet windy & Cold day – Enemy bombarded captured area several times during day – All areas Shelled – Casualties 1 Killed. 1 wounded – During Evening hostile counter attack was repulsed, sections getting direct targets. Strength of Coy – 11 off – 195 or –	ABS
	8/10/17	Mon	Dry & windy till Evening, then rain came on again heavily making the ground into a quagmire. Casualties ~~[illegible]~~ 4 (ABS) Killed ~~[illegible]~~ 5 (ABS) wounded – Transport Ration party had very rough journey –	ABS.

2353 Wt. W2544/1454 700,000 5/15 D. D. & L. A.D.S.S./Forms/C. 2118.

PAGE No 11

Instructions regarding War Diaries and Intelligence Summaries are contained in F. S. Regs., Part II. and the Staff Manual respectively. Title pages will be prepared in manuscript.

WAR DIARY of 147 MACHINE GUN COY or ~~INTELLIGENCE SUMMARY~~ for October 1917

(Erase heading not required.)

Army Form C. 2118.

Place	Date	Day	Summary of Events and Information	Remarks and references to Appendices
ZONNEBEKE SECTOR (Contd)	8/10/17	Mon	Transport warned in the night at 1.15am to take 16 pack animals to SPREE FARM by 5am – to act as mobile MG ammunition carriers – These left soon after 2am & arrived back at 2pm. Dark raining & windy throughout the night. Troops experienced great difficulty getting into assembly formations. Sections remained in the line with the exception of No 1. who withdrew to Coy HQ, arriving at about 3.50 am next day, wet & tired. A bad 24 hours, hostile artillery very active. During evening hostile attack was repulsed with loss to the enemy, who did not reach our lines – Strength of Coy 11 off 186 or –	AnS Lt
	9/10/17	Tues	Weather cleared towards morning, & day was quite good & dry. Rain during evening & night. Zero hour was fixed for 5.20am – Assaulting troops moved forward at that time. At 6am "Red Line" was reported captured. Hostile barrage dropped very heavily on KOREK area. At 9.35am OC Coy ordered Lt Hall with No 2 Secn to move to DAD trench to fire across the front of 66 Divn who were evidently held up – At 10am OC ordered No 4 Secn to move forward to PETER PAN. Hostile counter attack was repulsed during afternoon – Enemy kept up a shelling throughout the day but except for KOREK & another place it was very blind & disorganized. Strength of Coy 11 off 181 or –	AnS Lt

2353 Wt. W2544/1454 700,000 5/15 D. D. & L. A.D.S.S./Forms/C. 2118.

Report on Action of the 141st Company Machine Gun Corps during the Operations of the 9th Oct 1917

Army Form C. 2118.

WAR DIARY or INTELLIGENCE SUMMARY.

(Erase heading not required.)

Instructions regarding War Diaries and Intelligence Summaries are contained in F. S. Regs., Part II. and the Staff Manual respectively. Title pages will be prepared in manuscript.

Place	Date	Hour	Summary of Events and Information	Remarks and references to Appendices
W of PASSCHENDAELE	9/10/17		Ref Map During the evening of the 8th orders were received ordering the M Guns of the 141 M G Coy to remain in their present positions (distributed along the Div Front) & hold the present British line with the exception of No 1 Section (3 Guns) who withdrew to SPREE FARM at 2 a.m. thereby becoming Reserve Section. (This section had been holding the line in the 66th Div area) At 9 25 am on the 9th inst orders were received to send 1 Section Machine Guns to DAD TRENCH D 10 b 6 8., or nearest, to fire across the front of 66th Div & RAVEBEEK No 2 Section under command of LIEUT W. S. HART was ordered to carry out this operation. The Section (4 Guns) left the vicinity of BERLIN & WATERLOO Sq D 9 d proceeding by teams in extended order via the ground both sides of the GRAVENSTAFEL - BELLEVUE ROAD. When in vicinity of ROAD JUNCTION Sq D 10 a the Section came under a heavy hostile Machine Gun fire suffering several casualties, 2 Guns only getting through. (Fire came from direction of WOLF COPSE (D 4 c)) On getting to vicinity of MARSH BOTTOM Sq 10 a 90 40. the section re organized, a delay of about ½ hour being caused by having to send back & get gun equipment from those who had become casualties. About 2 pm the section (2 Guns) moved forward again & finally came into action in the vicinity of D 10 b 60 60 at about 3 pm. remaining there until orders to withdraw on relief of Div. The section did not open fire owing to the obscure situation on the front of the 66th Div At 9 35 am orders were received to Move 1 Section Machine Guns to PETER PAN D 4 c 3 3	

2353 Wt. W2544/1454 700,000 5/15 D. D. & L. A.D.S.S./Forms/C. 2118.

(2) Continued

Instructions regarding War Diaries and Intelligence Summaries are contained in F. S. Regs., Part II. and the Staff Manual respectively. Title pages will be prepared in manuscript.

WAR DIARY
or
INTELLIGENCE SUMMARY.
(Erase heading not required.)

Army Form C. 2118.

Place	Date	Hour	Summary of Events and Information	Remarks and references to Appendices
W of PASSCHENDAELE	9/10/17		No 4 Section under Command of Capt C W G BAIRD was ordered to carry out this operation. The Section (4 Guns) moved from the vicinity of Sq D 9 a 0 5 & proceeded direct to PETER PAN. They successfully passed through the hostile barrage N of CALGARY GRANGE, getting 3 casualties only & came into action (4 Guns) at PETER PAN about 3 pm. The guns were at once put into dispositions to cover front & flanks of that area & supply of ammunition arranged & got up. About 5 pm hostile counter attack was observed in motion, several parties of about 12 strong each being observed in area between BELLEVUE & DAD TRENCH. Section opened fire & casualties were inflicted on at least one party of the enemy. After 5.30 pm all was quiet in the area & no further hostile movement observed. During the day the Section in the vicinity of KOREK moved to new position near the old Boche front line to avoid the hostile barrage which was particularly violent along the KOREK Ridge. During the early hours of the 11th inst the Section withdrew to SPREE FARM as the infantry in that sector were relieved. The assembly of the Company in X Camp was completed at 8 am 11th inst. I beg to attach a list of Names of those whose conduct throughout the period was worthy of special mention. [signature] Capt	

2353 Wt. W2544/1454 700,000 5/15 D. D. & L. A.D.S.S./Forms/C. 2118.

Page 12.

Instructions regarding War Diaries and Intelligence Summaries are contained in F. S. Regs., Part II. and the Staff Manual respectively. Title Pages will be prepared in manuscript.

WAR DIARY or ~~INTELLIGENCE SUMMARY~~ of 144 Company MACHINE Gun Corps for OCTOBER 1914

(*Erase heading not required.*)

Army Form C. 2118.

Place	Date	~~Hour~~ Day	Summary of Events and Information	Remarks and references to Appendices
W of PASSCHENDAELE	10/10/14	Wed	Company engaged holding the captured line. Heavy hostile shelling & sniping throughout the day. At 10pm company began to withdraw from line with Infantry on relief of Division by N.Z Division. Relief was much hampered by hostile shelling & rain. At M.N Withdrawal had not been completed	[initials]
X CAMP ST JEAN	11/10/14	Thurs	A wet day. Withdrawal of Coy from line & assembly at ST JEAN completed at 8 am. During the afternoon the fit men of the company volunteered as stretcher bearers to fetch in wounded. Reorganization of Company commenced. Total losses during operations from 6th to 10th inst were Killed 16 O.R, Wounded 26, Evacuated Sick 12. A total of 54 other ranks thus became in-effective. During the night hostile planes dropped bombs in the vicinity of the Camp. otherwise quiet	[initials]
X Camp ST JEAN	12/10/14	Frid	Another Wet Day. Company Remained at ST JEAN. Transport arrived from VLAMATINGE. Company again volunteered & acted as Stretcher Bearers. Hostile planes again active & also a H.V gun which shelled the vicinity of the camp at irregular intervals throughout the day. Sick Nil Casualties Nil. Brigade in immediate Corps Reserve.	[initials]
X Camp ST JEAN	13/10/14	Sat	A wet day. Company engaged as Stretcher Bearers throughout the day. Hostile Planes active throughout day & night otherwise uneventful 24 hours. Sick Nil Casualties Nil.	[initials]
X CAMP ST JEAN	14/10/14	Sun	A dull day, rain towards evening & night. Company engaged cleaning up & Reorganizing. CAPT C.W.C BAIN to England on Duty. 2/Lt W A Hawes joined Coy from Base Depot. Hostile aerial activity throughout 24 hrs. Sick Nil Casualties Nil	[initials]

Page 13.

Instructions regarding War Diaries and Intelligence Summaries are contained in F. S. Regs., Part II. and the Staff Manual respectively. Title Pages will be prepared in manuscript.

WAR DIARY
~~or~~
~~INTELLIGENCE SUMMARY~~
(Erase heading not required.)

of 144th Company Machine Gun Corps for October 1914.

Army Form C. 2118.

Place	Date	Hour	Summary of Events and Information	Remarks and references to Appendices
X Camp St Jean	15/10/14	Mon.	A change in the weather, dry & fine throughout the day. A quiet day, Company engaged in reorganising & cleaning up. All lost & damaged gear replaced. Desultory shelling of area by a H.V gun during evening. Sick Nil. Casualties Nil.	[illegible]
Vlamertinghe Area 3	16/10/14	Tues	A fine morning. Company moved from St Jean to Hutments in No 3 area Vlamertinghe. rejoining 198th Bde 66 Div. Arrived & settled down by 2 pm. Hostile aerial activity throughout the 24 hours. Sick Nil Casualties Nil.	[illegible]
Vlamertinghe Area 3	17/10/14	Wed	A fine day, Rain during evening & throughout the night. Hostile aerial activity during day & night. Company engaged cleaning gear & limbers etc. Sick Nil Casualties Nil	[illegible]
– do –	18/10/14	Thurs	A fine day. Continued aerial activity of enemy. Company engaged in Elementary Gun Work. A quiet uneventful 24 hours. Sick Nil. Casualties Nil. Strength of Coy 11 offrs (9 Present, 1 leave, 1 Sick) 180 Other Ranks (166 Present, 4 leave, 2 Coy Inst, 2 Sick, 3 Reinforcement Camp)	[illegible]
– do –	19/10/14	Fri	A fine day, cold & dry. Training Resumed. Hostile aerial activity. Lt. Bo[illegible] & 3 O.Rs to leave. Sick Nil Casualties Nil. Strength of Coy 11 offrs (8 Present, 2 leave, 1 Sick) 180 OR. (7 leave, 2 Coy I, 2 Sick, 3 Rc)	[illegible]
– do –	20/10/14	Sat	A fine day, cold & dry. Training Resumed. Bombs dropped in vicinity of Camp during night. Sick Nil Casualties Nil. 1 Man Returned to Bn. Strength of Coy 11 offrs 149 other Ranks	[illegible]
– do –	21/10/14	Sun	A fine day. Rain throughout the night. Company to Divine Service. Throughout the night hostile planes were again active. Fired 1000 Rds without visible results. Sick Nil, Casualties Nil. Strength of Coy 11 offrs 149 O.R.	[illegible]
– do –	22/10/14	Mon	A fine morning, rather misty. Completion of Bathing at Vlamertinghe. Company resumed Training. O.C. Coy to Bde HQ as to be introduced to New Div Commdr. Lt Measor to Signal Course. A quiet uneventful 24 hours. Sick Nil. Casualties Nil. Strength of Coy 11 offrs (2 leave, 1 Sick, 8 Present) 149 Other Rks. (4 leave, 2 Sick, 3 Course of Instn, 3 Rein[illegible] Camp, Present 165)	[illegible]

2449 Wt. W14957/M90 750,000 1/16 J.B.C. & A. Forms/C.2118/12.

PAGE 14.

Instructions regarding War Diaries and Intelligence Summaries are contained in F. S. Regs., Part II. and the Staff Manual respectively. Title pages will be prepared in manuscript.

WAR DIARY of 147th Company/ MACHINE GUN CORPS

~~or INTELLIGENCE SUMMARY.~~

(Erase heading not required.)

for OCTOBER 1917.

Army Form C. 2118.

Place	Date	~~Hour~~ Day	Summary of Events and Information	Remarks and references to Appendices
VLAMERTINGHE Area 3	23/10/17	Tues	A dull, wet day. Company engaged Training. 2 N.C.O's to Div Gas School 5. O.R. to leave U.K. 1 O.R. to F.A. Sick. A quiet uneventful 24 hours. Sick 1. Casualties Nil. Strength of Coy 11 offrs 149 other Rks	J.M. Capt
-do-	24/10/17	Wed	A fine forenoon, Rain during afternoon & throughout night. Company paraded at 2 pm, embussed near VLAMERTINGHE at 2.30 pm & proceeded to WINNEZEELE area arriving at 6 pm. Billeting completed partly Barns & partly Tents. Sick Nil Casualties Nil. Strength of Coy 11 offrs 149 other Rks, distribution as follows. Offrs Present 8 Sick 1 leave 2. Other Rks Present 156 leave 11, Cox Inst 4 Sick 3, R.C. 4, Absent 1	J.M. Capt
WINNEZEELE	25/10/17	Thurs	A fine day strong dry wind. Company engaged cleaning up. Billets visited by G.O.C. Bde during forenoon. Sick Nil Casualties Nil. A quiet uneventful 24 hours. Strength of Coy 11 offrs 204 other Ranks. (25 Reinforcements from Base to Re. Camp)	J.M. Capt
WINNEZEELE	26/10/17	Frid	A wet day, cold. Company resumed Training. 2/Lt COATES to STEENVOORDE Billeting. A quiet uneventful 24 hours. Sick Nil. Casualties Nil	J.M. Capt
WINNEZEELE	27/10/17	Sat	A fine day, dry cold wind. Company moved from WINNEZEELE to STEENVOORDE Area West left 10 am arrived 11-15 am. Casualties en Route Nil. A quiet uneventful 24 hours. Sick Nil Casualties Nil. Strength of Coy 11 offrs 203 O.R.	J.M. Capt
STEENVOORDE	28/10/17		A fine day. Divine service during forenoon, limber Work during afternoon. Cpt Isherwood to F.A. Sick, L/C Pennington from Base to R.Camp. A quiet uneventful 24 hrs. Strength of Coy 11 offrs 204 O.R. Distribution as follows. Offrs 8 Present 2 leave, 1 Sick. Other Rks 153 Present, 12 leave, 5 Cox Inst, 3 F.A. 30 Reinforcement Camp.	J.M. Capt

2353 Wt. W2544/1454 700,000 5/15 D. D. & L. A.D.S.S./Forms/C. 2118.

PAGE 15/

Instructions regarding War Diaries and Intelligence Summaries are contained in F. S. Regs., Part II. and the Staff Manual respectively. Title pages will be prepared in manuscript.

WAR DIARY of 14th COMPANY MACHINE GUN CORPS.
or
~~INTELLIGENCE SUMMARY.~~
(Erase heading not required.)

for OCTOBER 1914.

Army Form C. 2118.

Place	Date	~~Hour~~ Day	Summary of Events and Information	Remarks and references to Appendices
STEENVOORDE	29/10/14	Mon	A fine day. Very cold & dry. Company resumed Training throughout the day. Lt SLATER rejoined from Leave. All Men at Reinforcement Camp joined company during forenoon. A quiet uneventful 24 hours. Sick Nil. Casualties Nil. Strength of Coy 11 Offrs 206 other Ranks.	J.M. Capt
STEENVOORDE	30/10/14	Tues	A showery day, cold. Guns of No 1 Section to Div Armourer for overhaul. Company carried on Training. Pte Anderson to F.A. Sick. A quiet uneventful 24 hours in Billet area. Sick 1. Casualties Nil. Strength of Company 11 Offrs 206 Other Ranks. Distribution of Personnel Officers Present 9 Leave 1 Sick 1. Other Ranks. Present 181. Leave 18. Courses of Instn 2 Sick F.A.H. Sick in U.K. 1	J.M. Capt

In the Field
31.10.14

J. M[illegible] Capt
Commdg 14th Coy Machine Gun Corps.

2353 Wt. W2544/1454 700,000 5/15 D. D. & L. A.D.S.S./Forms/C. 2118.

Vol 23

S E C R E T.

WAR DIARY

OF

147th Mach Gun Coy

FOR

November 1917

PAGE.16.

Instructions regarding War Diaries and Intelligence Summaries are contained in F. S. Regs., Part II. and the Staff Manual respectively. Title pages will be prepared in manuscript.

WAR DIARY of 144th Company ~~or INTELLIGENCE SUMMARY.~~ MACHINE GUN CORPS.

(Erase heading not required.)

for NOVEMBER 1914.

Army Form C. 2118.

Place	Date	~~Hour~~ Day	Summary of Events and Information	Remarks and references to Appendices
STEENVORDE	31/10/14	Wed	A fine day, dry & warm. Company resumed Training throughout the day. Lt BOXER returned from leave. Cpl SHERWOOD to C.C.S. Struck off Strength. 5 O.R to leave U.K. Lt HANAGHAN to Bailleul to attend a Lecture. All other Officers & N.C.O's to Lecture on "Strategy" during the afternoon. Company to Baths. Sick Nil. Casualties Nil. Strength of Coy 11 offrs 206 other Rks. A quiet uneventful 24 hours.	[illegible] Capt
STEENVORDE	1/11/14	Thurs.	Officers on Strength of Coy on 1-11-14. Capt J. MOHLIG M.C Commdg Coy. Lt A.B. SELLMAN 2/in Command. Lt W.J. HAIN M.C Commdg No 2 Section. Lt H.S. BOXER Commdg No 3 Section. Lieut P.A HANAGHAN Commdg No 4 Sect. 2/Lt H SMITH Commdg No 1 Section. Lieut W.J. SLATER No 1 Section. 2/Lt W.A HAWES No 2 Section. 2/Lt W.S COATES No 3 Sectn. Capt G.C WOODS Transport Offr. Lieut J.S. PHILLIPS Base Sick. Coy Sgt Maj A. MITCHELL. Coy QMSgt H SYKES. A fine day, cold & dry. 8 Military Medals awarded to N.C.O's & men of the Company. Remainder of Coy to Baths during early morning. Sgt Gough to Div Gas School. 9 O.R from Base joined Company. Pt Read rejoined from leave. Sick Nil, Casualties Nil. Strength of Coy 11 offrs 214 other Ranks distributed Offrs Present 10 Sick Base 1. O.R Present 185 leave 22, Sick 3, Courses of Instn 3, Absent 1.	[illegible] Capt
STEENVORDE	2/11/14	Fri	A fine day, rather overcast. Lt Hall to F.A Sick. Company resumed Training. Sick & Casualties Nil. A quiet uneventful 24 hours. Strength of Coy 11 offrs 214 O.R	[illegible] Capt
STEENVORDE	3/11/14	Sat.	A fine day. Training resumed. Coy visited by Div Commdr during forenoon. Sick Nil. Casualties Nil. A quiet uneventful 24 hrs. 3 O.R returned from leave. Strength of Coy 11 offrs 214 O.Ranks.	[illegible] Capt

2353 Wt. W2544/1454 700,000 5/15 D. D. & L. A.D.S.S./Forms/C. 2118.

PAGE 14

Instructions regarding War Diaries and Intelligence Summaries are contained in F. S. Regs., Part II. and the Staff Manual respectively. Title pages will be prepared in manuscript.

WAR DIARY of 144th Company / Machine Gun Corps
~~or INTELLIGENCE SUMMARY~~ for NOVEMBER 1917

(Erase heading not required.)

Army Form C. 2118.

Place	Date	~~Hour~~ Day	Summary of Events and Information	Remarks and references to Appendices
STEENVOORDE.	4/11/17	Sun	A fair day, cold. Company to Divine Service during forenoon. Inspection of Gas appliances by Div Gas N Co during afternoon. Sick Nil Casualties Nil A quiet uneventful 24 hours Strength of Coy 11 Offrs 214 Other Ranks Distribution as follows. Offrs Present 9, Sick 2. Other Ranks Present 188, Leave 18, Coy D. 3, Sick 5.	[illegible] Capt
" "	5/11/17	Mon	A fine day. Training resumed. Visited during forenoon by Col. Bateman (Act Brigadier) Capt J. Mulley M.C. proceeded on leave to U.K. + 6 O.R. Capt G. C. Foulds assumed command of the Coy. ~~[illegible]~~ Strength of Coy 11 Offs + 212 O.R. distributed as follows. Offs present 8. Sick 2 Leave 1. Other Ranks present 184. Leave 20 Coy D. 3 Sick 5	[illegible] Capt
" "	6/11/17	Tues	A wet morning. Training resumed. Visited during morning by the D.A.V.S. who inspected all animals. A quiet uneventful 24 hours. Strength of Coy. 11 Offrs - 212 other ranks. Distribution as follows:- Offrs Present 8 leave 1 Sick 2. Other ranks Present 185. leave 19. sick 4. Coy D. 4.	[illegible] Capt
" "	7/11/17	WED	A fine day, but misty morning. Training resumed. No I Section reported to C.O. 1/4th W. R. Regt + practiced "BATT. in ATTACK". Sgt TURNER gave instruction to Offrs + N.C.O.s of 1/6 W. R. Regt on the German Machine Gun. Offrs attended lecture at STEENVOORDE by Area Commdt. Subject "BATTLES of VERDUN". 1 O.R. reinforcement arrived	

PAGE 18.

Instructions regarding War Diaries and Intelligence Summaries are contained in F. S. Regs., Part II. and the Staff Manual respectively. Title pages will be prepared in manuscript.

WAR DIARY or INTELLIGENCE SUMMARY. of 147th Company MACHINE GUN CORPS for NOVEMBER 1917

(Erase heading not required.)

Army Form C. 2118.

Place	Date	~~Hour~~ Day	Summary of Events and Information	Remarks and references to Appendices
STEENVOORDE	7/11/17	WED	All attached men + latest draft fired on range. A quiet uneventful 24 hours Strength of Coy. 11 Offrs + 213 Other Ranks, Distribution as follows. Offr Present 8 leave 1 Sick 2. Other ranks Present 186, leave 19 C of D. 3 Sick 5.	[illegible]
"	8/11/17	THUR	A wet day Training resumed. No 3 Section reported to O C 1/6th W.R. Regt + practiced BATT in ATTACK Sgt TORNER gave instruction to Offrs + N C Os of 1/7th W.R. Regt on the German Machine Gun Coy prepared for move (9th inst) A quiet uneventful 24 hours Strength of Coy 11 Offrs + 213 Other Ranks Distributed as follows. Offr Present 8. leave 1. Sick 2. Other ranks present 183 leave 22 C of D. 3 Sick 5.	[illegible]
"	9/11/17	FRID	A fine day. Coy moved to DICKEBUSCH area, + took over billets vacated by 7th Australian M G C (Map Ref H18 c 2 1) sheet 28 1/40,000. Coy moved by busses from STEENVOORDE followed by 4 mile march to billets, arriving at 7-30 pm. Transport moved independently arriving at 3-30 pm Strength of Coy 11 Offr + 213 Other Ranks Distribution as follows. Offr Present 8, leave 1. sick 2. Other Ranks Present 182 leave 22 sick 6. C of D 3	[illegible]

2353 Wt. W2544/1454 700,000 5/15 D. D. & L. A.D.S.S./Forms/C. 2118.

PAGE 19.

Instructions regarding War Diaries and Intelligence Summaries are contained in F. S. Regs., Part II. and the Staff Manual respectively. Title pages will be prepared in manuscript.

WAR DIARY or INTELLIGENCE SUMMARY.

(Erase heading not required.)

of 147 COMPANY. MACHINE GUN CORPS for NOVEMBER 1917.

Army Form C. 2118.

Place	Date	~~Hour~~ Day	Summary of Events and Information	Remarks and references to Appendices
CANAL AREA	10/11/17	SAT.	A very wet day. Coy remained at camp H18 C21. 2 Other ranks struck off strength 1. O.R proceeded on C of S. Strength of Coy 11 Offrs + 211 Other ranks, distributed as follows Off Present 8. leave 1. sick 2. Other ranks present 179. leave 22. C of S 4. sick 6. 1. L.D horse on strength of Coy.	G.L.P. Capt
" "	11/11/17	SUN.	A fine day, with occasional showers. Coy carried on training in huts. an uneventful 24 hours, Strength of Coy 11 Off 211 Other ranks. Distributed as follows. Off Present 8. leave 1. Sick 2. Other ranks Present 181. leave 20. C of S 4 Sick 6.	G.L.P. Capt
" "	12/11/17	MON	A fine day. Training resumed in huts owing to state of camp. Uneventful 24 hours, Strength of Coy 11 Offrs + 208 Other ranks. Distributed as follows. - Off Present 8 leave 1, sick 2. Other ranks present, 184, leave 17 C of S 3. sick 4.	G.L.P. Capt
"	13/11/17	TUES.	A fine day. Training resumed. Uneventful 24 hours Strength of Coy. 11 Offrs + 207 Other Ranks distributed as follows Off Present 8. leave 1. sick 2. Other Ranks Present 179 leave 21 C of S 3 sick 4 4. O.R. proceeded on leave to U.K 1 N.C.O to C.C.S + struck off strength accordingly.	G.L.P. Capt

PAGE 20.

Instructions regarding War Diaries and Intelligence Summaries are contained in F. S. Regs., Part II. and the Staff Manual respectively. Title pages will be prepared in manuscript.

WAR DIARY of 147 COMPANY. or INTELLIGENCE SUMMARY. MACHINE GUN CORPS for NOVEMBER 1917

(Erase heading not required.)

Army Form C. 2118.

Place	Date	~~Hour~~ Day	Summary of Events and Information	Remarks and references to Appendices
Canal Area	14/11/17	WED.	A misty day but training resumed. Lt M F KINDER joined Co + taken on strength. Uneventful 24 hours. Strength of Co 12 Offrs + 207 Other Ranks distributed as follows: Offrs Present 9 leave 1 sick 2. Other ranks Present 180. leave 20. C of S. 3 sick 4.	[illegible]
" "	15/11/17	THURS	A fine day. Training resumed. Lt BOXER reconnoitred the line to be taken over. Uneventful 24 hours. Strength of Co 12 Offrs + 205 Other Ranks distributed as follows:- Offrs Present 9. leave 1. sick 2. Other Ranks present 178. leave 20. C of S 3 sick 4. Cpl MEYER under A.G. authority to U.K. on special course. 1 L.D. horse sent to Mobile Vet Section.	[illegible]
" "	16/11/17	FRI	A fine day. Training resumed. CAPT. FOULDS + all section Officers reconnoitred the line to be taken over. Uneventful 24 hours. 1 L.D. horse struck off strength of Co. Strength of Co 12 Offrs + 205 other ranks distributed as follows:- Offrs Present 9. leave 1. sick 2. Other Ranks present 182. leave 16 C of S 3. sick 4.	[illegible]
" "	17/11/17	SAT.	A fine day. Co had baths at YPRES. Lt KINDER. 2/Lt COATES + 3 N.C.Os reconnoitred the line to be taken over. Uneventful 24 hours. Strength of Co 12 Offrs + 168 Other Ranks	

Instructions regarding War Diaries and Intelligence Summaries are contained in F. S. Regs., Part II. and the Staff Manual respectively. Title pages will be prepared in manuscript.

WAR DIARY
or
INTELLIGENCE SUMMARY.
(Erase heading not required.)

of 147 COMPANY MACHINE GUN CORPS for NOVEMBER 1917

Army Form C. 2118.

Place	Date	~~Hour~~ DAY	Summary of Events and Information	Remarks and references to Appendices
Ypres Area	17/11/17	SAT.	Attached men from Batts were returned to their respective units viz 36. under 49th DIV. Authority Ga 76/3. Strength of Coy present 9 Off leave 1, sick 2. Other Ranks present 143. leave 19. Coy T 3, sick 3.	[illegible]
"	18/11/17	Sun-	Fine day. Three Secns of 147 MGC relieved corresponding number of 146 MGC. in line. Coy. HQ situated at J 4 b 76.55. (Sheet 28) No 1 Secn + 1 gun team from No 4 took over barrage posns. No 3 Secn in right Sector No 4 left Sector. Relief complete 7 30 pm. No 2 Secn remained at BELGIAN BATTERY CAMP under Lieut Slater – Officers in line Capt Foulds Lt Smith Lt Boxer Lt Hanaghan + Lt Kinder – At 8.30 pm Capt Foulds sent word for 2 Lt Coates to be sent up to Coy HQ. Lt Hanaghan came down to BELGIAN BATTERY Camp during evening sick. Strength of Coy 12 off 168 or. Lt Smith fired 1500 rounds harrassing fire on targets given by DMGO. Gas shells sent over by enemy during night – Casualties nil.	[illegible]
"	19/11/17	Mon.	Fine Day. No 1 Secn. fired 2500 R. indirect overhead on selected targets – No 4 Secn. fired 2000 R. indirect overhead on selected targets – One team of No 4 Secn. was heavily shelled by gas shells	[illegible]

A. B. Sellman Lieut

Page 22

Instructions regarding War Diaries and Intelligence Summaries are contained in F. S. Regs., Part II. and the Staff Manual respectively. Title pages will be prepared in manuscript.

WAR DIARY of 147 M. G. Coy.

or

~~INTELLIGENCE SUMMARY.~~ for November 1917.

(Erase heading not required.)

Army Form C. 2118.

Place	Date	~~Hour~~ Day	Summary of Events and Information	Remarks and references to Appendices
CANAL AREA	19/11/17	Mon	having to wear their box respirators from 10 pm – midnight. Neighbourhood of Coy HQ heavily shelled from 8 pm – midnight. DMGO made special survey of line, & stayed night at Coy HQ. Work done on barrage positions which were slightly improved. Night firing position made. Strength of Coy 12 offs 168 or	[illegible]
"	20/11/17	Tues.	Fine day. Evans No 4 Secn. badly blistered by shell gas on hands, sent to 1/6 WRR aid post. Pts Chidgey & Bramley were slightly gassed & reported sick at Coy HQ. From 2-4 pm. Enemy heavily shelled No 1 barrage position with guns of a heavy calibre. No 1 Secn. fired 2750 rounds on selected enemy trench tracks. Telephone wire from Coy. H.Q. to No 4 Secn broken by enemy shell fire. Strength of Coy 12 offs 168 or. – Casualties 1. Evans.	[illegible]
– do –	21/11/17	Wed	A fine day, heavy hostile shelling of front area during 24 hours. Guns in line fired 6000 Rds during the night on selected Targets. Neighbourhood of Coy HQ Qrs shelled. Sick Nil. Casualties Nil. Lt Phillips to U K Struck off strength	[illegible]
– do –	22/11/17	Thurs	A fine day. Gas shelling of Front Area during the night. Guns in line fired 3500 Rds. Sick 1 Casualties Nil.	[illegible]
– do –	23/11/17	Frid	A fine day. A fairly quiet 24 hrs in the line. Guns fired 5500 Rds during the night. Sick Nil Casualties Nil	

2353 Wt. W2544/1454 700,000 5/15 D. D. & L. A.D.S.S./Forms/C. 2118.

Page 23.

Instructions regarding War Diaries and Intelligence Summaries are contained in F. S. Regs., Part II. and the Staff Manual respectively. Title pages will be prepared in manuscript.

WAR DIARY of 144th Coy MACHINE Gun Corps

or

~~INTELLIGENCE SUMMARY.~~

(*Erase heading not required.*)

for NOVEMBER 1914

Army Form C. 2118.

Place	Date	~~Hour~~ Day	Summary of Events and Information	Remarks and references to Appendices
Trenches BEELAERT Sector	24/11/14	Sat	A fine day, very windy inclined to Rain. A quiet uneventful 24 hrs in the line Guns fired 6000 Rds during the night. Sick, Casualties Nil. Strength of Coy 11 Offs 166 Other Ranks	[illegible] Capt
-- do --	25/11/14	Sun	A fine day very windy & day. Rain during evening & night, very cold. A fairly quiet uneventful 24 hours in the Line. Sick Nil Casualties 1. O.R. Wounded (Shell fire) Guns in line fired [illegible]000 Rds on allotted Targets during night. Strength of Coy 11 Offs 166 Other Ranks	[illegible] Capt
-- do --	26/11/14	Mon	A fine day, windy & cold, Coy relieved 146 M G Coy in Barrage Positions during the day. 9 O.R to leave. [illegible] 8 OR from 254 Coy arrived for instruction. Rain throughout evening & night Sick Nil Casualties Nil Lt [illegible] to Base. Sick. A fairly quiet uneventful 24 hours Strength of Coy 10 Offs 166 O.R.	[illegible] Capt
-- do --	27/11/14	Tues	A wet day. No 3 Section resting at Transport Lines. Pte Wright 69 Self Inflicted Wound. Pte Wright B.E. Wounded Shell fire. Attached men of 254 Coy to the Line. Heavy artillery duel throughout the day & night. 4 O R from leave. Sick Nil Casualties 2 Strength of Coy 10 offs 164 O. R.	[illegible] Capt
-- do --	28/11/14	Wed	A fine day. Hostile artillery action throughout 24 hrs. Otherwise a quiet 24 hours. Sick Nil. Casualties Nil. Lt Hall Struck off Strength. [illegible] Strength 9 offs 162 O.R.	[illegible] Capt
-- do --	29/11/14	Thurs	A fine day. Hostile artillery action throughout the day. Otherwise a quiet uneventful day. Sick Nil, Casualties Nil Strength of Coy 9 offs 140 O.R. 8 OR from Base. Distribution Offs 4 Present 2 leave. O.R. 130 Present 33 leave, 4 Cyl, 3 Fld amb.	[illegible] Capt

[illegible] 30.11.14

[illegible] Capt Commdg 144 M G Coy.

2353 Wt. W2544/1454 700,000 5/15 D. D. & L. A.D.S.S./Forms/C. 2118.

Instructions regarding War Diaries and Intelligence Summaries are contained in F. S. Regs., Part II, and the Staff Manual respectively. Title pages will be prepared in manuscript.

WAR DIARY
or
INTELLIGENCE SUMMARY.

(*Erase heading not required.*)

Army Form C. 2118.

Place	Date	Hour	Summary of Events and Information	Remarks and references to Appendices
			W A R D I A R Y.	
			o f	
			1 4 7 th M A C H I N E G U N C O M P A N Y.	
			for month of	
			D E C E M B E R 1 9 1 7.	

D. D. & L., London, E.C.
(A7883) Wt. W2o7/M1672 350,000 4/17 Sch. 52a Forms/C/2118/14

PAGE 24.

Instructions regarding War Diaries and Intelligence Summaries are contained in F. S. Regs., Part II. and the Staff Manual respectively. Title pages will be prepared in manuscript.

WAR DIARY

or

~~INTELLIGENCE SUMMARY.~~

(Erase heading not required.)

of 144th Company MACHINE GUN CORPS. for DECEMBER 1917

Army Form C. 2118.

Place	Date	~~Hour~~ Day	Summary of Events and Information	Remarks and references to Appendices
TRENCHES BECELAERE Sector	30/11/17	Frid	A dull morning inclined to Rain. Hostile artillery active against Back areas throughout the 24 hours. Sick Nil. Casualties Lt. J.S. SLATER wounded by Shell fire. Otherwise a quiet & uneventful 24 hrs. Strength of Coy 8 officers 169 Other Rks. Pte [illegible] to CCS.	[signature]
- do -	1/12/17	Sat	A cold day, windy & inclined to rain. Officers on Strength of Coy on 1st December 17 Capt. J. MUNRO M.C Commdg Coy. Lieut A.B. SELLMAN 2/in Command (Leave U.K.) Capt G.C. POULOS Transport Offr. 2/Lt H SMITH Commdg No. 1 Section (on leave) 2/Lt W.S. COATES Commdg No 2 Section Lt H.S. BOXER —"— No 3 —"— Lt G.J. KINDER —"— No 4 —"— 2/Lt W.A. HAWES No 2 —"— Preparation for forthcoming operations were prepared & completed during the days. A fairly quiet 24 hours in the line, hostile artillery rather active during day. Sick Nil. Casualties Nil, Strength of Coy 8 officers 169 Other Rks. Distributions as follows. Officers Present 6 Leave 2. Other Rks Present 132. Leave 32 C of D 3 Sick F.A. 2.	[signature]
- do -	2/12/17	Sun	A cold day, very windy. 4 O.R to Leave. Rain during evening, sharp frost during night. A fairly quiet 24 hours in the line. No 3 Section to A Battery during the night. Pt Hudson to F.A Sick. Pt Oldham to C.C.S. Struck off. Sick 1. Casualties Nil. Strength of Coy 8 offrs 168 Other Ranks.	[signature]
- do -	3/12/17	Mon	A cold day, very windy. Attached O.R of 264 Coy rejoined their Coy. A fairly quiet 24 hours. Guns fired 40000 Rds in connection with operations of New Zealand Division against POLDERHOEK CHATEAU. Sick Nil. Casualties Nil. Strength of Coy 8 offrs 168 Other Ranks.	[signature]
- do -	4/12/17	Tues	A cold day. Snow fell during day. Pt Bows to Chiropodist Course. A quiet uneventful 24 hours in line. During the night B Batty & Coy H.Q. Ors were relieved by 148 Coy. Section returned to Billets by 12 m.n. Sick Nil. Casualties Nil. Strength of Coy 8 offrs 166 Other Ranks.	[signature]

A5834 Wt. W4973/M687 750,000 8/16 D. D. & L. Ltd. Forms/C.2118/13.

PAGE 25

Instructions regarding War Diaries and Intelligence Summaries are contained in F. S. Regs., Part II. and the Staff Manual respectively. Title Pages will be prepared in manuscript.

WAR DIARY

or

~~INTELLIGENCE SUMMARY~~

(Erase heading not required.)

of 144 Company Machine Gun Corps for December 1917

Army Form C. 2118.

Place	Date	~~Hour~~ Day	Summary of Events and Information	Remarks and references to Appendices
TRENCHES BECELAERE SECTOR	5/12/17	Wed	A very cold day, frost during day. B Battery relieved by 254 MG Coy & returned to Billets. A quiet uneventful 24 hours. Sick Nil. 1 horse killed by Bomb in POPERINGE during evening. Sick Nil Casualties Nil. 4 O.R. from leave. Strength of Coy 8 offrs 166 other Ranks.	[illegible]
TRENCHES BECELAERE SECTOR	6/12/17	Thur	A cold day, frost. Company to YPRES BATHS. returned no baths. 3 other Rks to leave. A quiet uneventful 24 hours except for a little Bomb dropping during early hours of night. Casualties Nil. Sick Nil. Strength of Coy 8 offrs 166 Other Ranks	[illegible]
Reserve Billet DICKEBUSCH area	7/12/17	Frid	A mild day. Capt Tadds & 2 O.R. to Cannes. 4 O.R. from Base. Sections cleaning up & reorganizing. 3 O.Rs to leave. A quiet uneventful 24 hours. Sick Nil. Casualties Nil. Strength of Coy. 8 offrs 140 other Ranks.	[illegible]
- do -	8/12/17	Sat	A fair day, mild, but heavy rain during early hours. 4 O.Rs to leave. Company to Baths during forenoon. Improvements in Billets carried out. Lt Ward joined Coy from Base Depot. Lt Sellman rejoined from leave. A quiet uneventful 24 hours. Sick Nil. Casualties Nil. Strength of Coy 9 offrs 142 other Ranks.	[illegible]
- do -	9/12/17	Sun	A wet & cold day. Sections work at Improving conditions of Billets. Pt Riley Struck off. A quiet uneventful 24 hours in Billet area. 3 O.Rs returned from leave. Sick Nil Casualties Nil. Strength of Coy 9 officers 141 other Ranks.	[illegible]
- do -	10/12/17	Mon	A fine forenoon. Company at work improving Billets. Lt Coates & Ward to Line for Reconnaissance. A fairly quiet uneventful 24 hrs. Sick Nil. Casualties Nil. Strength of Coy 9 offrs 141 other Ranks.	[illegible]
- do -	11/12/17	Tues	A fine day, very cold. Sections Preparing for the Line. Pt Cheek rejoined from CCS. 2/Lt Clarke from Base Depot. A quiet 24 hours. Sick Nil. Casualties Nil. Strength of Company 10 offrs 142 other Ranks.	[illegible]

2449 Wt. W14957/M90 750,000 1/16 J.B.C. & A. Forms/C.2118/12.

Page 26.

Instructions regarding War Diaries and Intelligence Summaries are contained in F. S. Regs., Part II. and the Staff Manual respectively. Title pages will be prepared in manuscript.

WAR DIARY of 147th Company Machine Gun Corps
or
INTELLIGENCE SUMMARY.
(Erase heading not required.)

for DECEMBER 1917

Army Form C. 2118.

Place	Date	Day	Summary of Events and Information	Remarks and references to Appendices
Rest Billets. DICKEBUSCH AREA	12/12/17	Wed.	A fine day. Sections preparing for move into the Line Pt Belgium to Hd Amb. Improvements carried out at Transport Lines. Strength of Coy 10 off 172 OR –	
ZONNEBEKE AREA	13/12/17	Thu.	Relief of 146 + 148 M.G. Coys completed at 6 am – In forward area ZONNEBEKE Sector. A fairly quiet day – Coy HQ shelled intermittently during day – Forward guns of No 1 Sec: heavily shelled whilst relief was proceeding. A quiet night – Casualties nil – Improvements at Camp (Rear HQ) proceeded with – Strength of Coy 11 off – 173 OR – Casualties nil	
"	14/12/17	Fri.	A fairly quiet day – Hostile artillery active on whole area – Strength of Coy. 10 off 173 OR – Casualties nil –	
"	15/12/17	Sat.	A fine day, bright – Hostile artillery very active throughout day – Area of Coy HQ heavily shelled from 12 noon to 4 pm with heavies – O.C. Coy. sited new forward positions for left forward guns – Strength of Coy 10 off: 173 OR – Casualties nil.	
"	16/12/17	Sun.	Cold but fine day – Heavy hostile shelling of all areas at intervals throughout the day – 2Lt Smith returned from leave – Sgt Turner (No 3 Sec) wounded – Strength of Coy 10 off – 172 OR –	
"	17/12/17	Mon.	Cold day. Snow during night. Hostile artillery fairly active throughout day. During night the left [illegible] was blown up & the team buried. All got quite straight. Sick Nil Casualties Nil. Strength of Coy 10 Offrs 171 Other Ranks.	
-do-	18/12/17	Tues	Cold day, [illegible] & mist throughout the day. A fairly quiet 24 hours. Artillery activity normal. Sgt [illegible] wounded during the evening. Sick Nil Casualties Nil. Strength of Coy 10 Offrs 171 Other Ranks	
-do-	19/12/17	Wed	A fine morning, very frosty. Coy relieved in the Line by 146 M.G. Coy. Relief completed without incident by 4 am. Sick Nil Casualties Nil. Strength of Coy 10 Officers 171 Other Ranks	
-do-	20/12/17	Thurs	A frosty day, heavy mist throughout the 24 hours. A quiet day in Billet area. Sick [illegible] Casualties Nil. Strength of Coy 10 Offrs 171 Other Ranks	

A5831 Wt W4973/M687 750,000 8/16 D. D. & L. Ltd. Forms/C.2118/13.

PAGE 24

Instructions regarding War Diaries and Intelligence Summaries are contained in F. S. Regs., Part II. and the Staff Manual respectively. Title Pages will be prepared in manuscript.

WAR DIARY of 147th Company MACHINE Gun CORPS for December 1917

~~or INTELLIGENCE SUMMARY~~

(Erase heading not required.)

Army Form C.

Place	Date	Hour	Summary of Events and Information	Remarks and references to Appendices
[illegible] Billets Belgian Battery Corner.	21/12/17	Fri	A quiet day in Billeting area. Thick mist & fog throughout the day. 2Lt Hyslop to [illegible] sick [illegible]. Strength of Coy 10 offs 171 Other Ranks	[illegible]
— do —	22/12/17	Sat.	Fine, cold day. Two Sections (Nos 1 + 4) relieved 148 M.G.C. in line (right Bgd: ZONNEBEKE Sector) Strength of Coy 10 offs 171 or.	[initials]
ZONNEBEKE Sector	23/12/17	Sun.	Fine day. Hard frost. Enemy artillery active over whole area. Strength of Coy 10 offs 171 or.	[initials]
"	24/12/17	Mon.	Snow + frost. Fairly quiet day in line. Secns in reserve training during day in huts. Strength of Coy. 10 off. 171 or. Pt. Swann (No 4 Secn) wounded.	[initials]
"	25/12/17	Tues	Fine, bright day. Normal day in line. Strength of Coy. 10 off. 170 or.	[initials]
"	26/12/17	Wed	Hard frost. Hostile artillery active during evening. Strength of Coy: 10 off. 170 or.	[initials]
"	27/12/17	Thrs.	Frost + Snow. Normal day in line. Strength of Coy. 10 off. 170 or.	[initials]
"	28/12/17	Fri.	Hard frost. Nos 2 + 3 Secns preparing for relief in line. Corp. Sanderson left for course at GRANTHAM. Pt Cheetham [?] sent to Base depot. sick. Strength of Coy. 10 off. 168 or.	[initials]
"	29/12/17	Sat.	Cold, fine day. Nos 2 + 3 Secns. relieved Nos 1 + 4 Secns in line. relief complete 7 pm.	[initials]
"	30/12/17	Sun.	Cold day. Usual hostile artillery activity over whole area. Strength of Coy. 10 off. 174 or. 6 reinforcements taken on strength.	[initials]

A. B. Sillman [?] Lt.

2449 Wt. W14957/M90 750,000 1/16 J.B.C. & A. Forms/C.2118/12.

Secret

War Diary

Vol 25

of

147 Mach Gun Coy

for

January /18

– 147 Inf: Bgd

Herewith Sheets 28 – 31
of War Diary for month
of January 1918 —

A. B. Sillman Lt
147 Machine Gun Coy.

PAGE 28 –

Army Form C. 2118.

WAR DIARY

~~or~~

~~INTELLIGENCE SUMMARY.~~

(*Erase heading not required.*)

147 Machine Gun Coy –

For – the month of January 1918

Instructions regarding War Diaries and Intelligence Summaries are contained in F. S. Regs., Part II. and the Staff Manual respectively. Title pages will be prepared in manuscript.

Place	Date	~~Hour~~ Day	Summary of Events and Information	Remarks and references to Appendices
ZONNEBEKE SECTOR	31/12/17	Mon–	A cold frosty day – Usual hostile artillery activity over whole area – Strength of Coy 10 off 174 OR.	ABS Lt.
"	1/1/18	Tues	A fine cold day – Enemy artillery active over whole area – Pt Cheek Killed in action – Pt Sullivan wounded in action (both No 3 Secn:) Strength of Coy 10 off 173 OR – Roll of officers – Capt. J. Muhlig M.C. Comm'g Coy. Lieut A. B. Sellman 2nd in Comm: 2nd Lieut. H. Smith OC No 1 Secn: Lieut T. Ward OC No 2 Secn. Lieut H. Boxer OC No 3 Secn 2nd Lieut W. S. Coates Sub Secn off No 3 – Capt M. F. Kinder OC No 4 Secn. 2nd Lieut A. H. Clark Sub Secn off No 4 Secn – 2 Lt W. A. Hawes acting T.O. Capt G. C. Foulds (hospital sick)	ABS Lt.
"	2/1/18	Wed	Fine cold day – Quiet 24 hrs in line – Strength of Coy: 10 off 170 OR –	ABS Lt.
"	3/1/18	Thrs	Cold frosty day – Usual hostile artillery activity over whole area. Strength of Coy. 10 off. 170 OR	ABS Lt.
"	4/1/18	Fri	Cold frosty day – Normal day in line – Pt Flanders from hospital BCCS. Strength of Coy 10 off 169 OR –	ABS Lt.
"	5/1/18	Sat	Cold day – Nos 2 & 3 Secns of 147 MGC relieved in line by C & D. Secns of 146 MGC relief complete by 5.30 pm. Strength of Coy 10 off 168 OR –	ABS Lt.
"	6/1/18	Sun –	Cold frosty day – Sections engaged in cleaning guns Equipment etc: Company went to YPRES baths Strength of Coy 10 off 168 OR –	ABS Lt.
"	7/1/18	Mon –	Slight break in frost – Company paid out – Sections spent morning sorting gun Equipment etc. Strength of Coy: 10 off 169 OR –	ABS Lt.
"	8/1/18	Tues	Cold day – Snow – Company preparing for move – Strength of Coy 10 off 169 OR –	ABS Lt.

A. B. Sellman Lieut
147 MGC.

A5834 Wt. W4973/M687 750,000 8/16 D. D. & L. Ltd. Forms/C.2118/13.

PAGE 29

Instructions regarding War Diaries and Intelligence Summaries are contained in F. S. Regs., Part II. and the Staff Manual respectively. Title pages will be prepared in manuscript.

WAR DIARY ~~or INTELLIGENCE SUMMARY.~~ of 147 Machine Gun Coy. For month of January 1918 -

(Erase heading not required.)

Army Form C. 2118.

Place	Date	~~Hour~~ Day.	Summary of Events and Information	Remarks and references to Appendices
ST MARIE CAPPEL area	9/1/18	Wed.	Company left Camp at BELGIAN BATTERY CORNER at 11 am. Embussed near OUDERDOM at 1.30 pm - arrived at ST MARIE CAPPEL at 5 pm after a bitterly cold journey in a Snow Storm. 2Lt Coates leave to UK. Strength of Coy. 10 off. 169 OR -	ABS Lt
"	10/1/18	Thrs.	Company straightening up limbers preparatory to moving to CAESTRE area. Coy. strength 10 off. 168 OR -	ABS Lt
CAESTRE area	11/1/18	Fri	Coy. moved to CAESTRE area. Moved off 9 am arrived billets at 10.45 am. Mild raining day. Billets good, but scattered. Strength of Coy. 10 off 168 OR -	ABS Lt
"	12/1/18	Sat	Mild fine day - Coy. engaged in cleaning up etc. in morning - Football practice in afternoon - Strength of Coy. 10 off: 167 OR -	ABS Lt
"	13/1/18	Sun	Coy training in morning - Inter-Section football competition started. No 3. 1 goal No 2 nil. Heavy Snow Storm in night - Strength of Coy. 10 off 167 OR -	ABS Lt
	14/1/18	Mon	Coy training in morning - Football. Transport 2 No 4 Secn 1. Strength of Coy 10 off 166 OR -	ABS Lt
	15/1/18	Tues.	Heavy Rain Storm all day. No 2 Secn billet flooded during night, & moved next day. O.C. Coy. reconnoitred range during ~~day~~ morning - Coy paid out - Strength of Coy 10 off 166 OR -	ABS Lt
	16/1/18	Wed.	Mild & raining day - Training proceeded with, but no football possible - Strength of Coy 10 off 166 OR -	ABS Lt

A.B. Sellman Lieut.
147 M.G.Coy.

PAGE 30

Instructions regarding War Diaries and Intelligence Summaries are contained in F. S. Regs., Part II. and the Staff Manual respectively. Title pages will be prepared in manuscript.

WAR DIARY of 147 Machine Gun Coy.

~~or~~

~~INTELLIGENCE SUMMARY.~~

(*Erase heading not required.*)

Army Form C. 2118.

Place	Date	~~Hour~~ Day	Summary of Events and Information	Remarks and references to Appendices
CAESTRE Area	17/1/18	Thrs.	Snow & rain. Company training – no football possible – Strength of Coy – 10 off – 171 OR – Coy Canteen opened at Coy HQ –	A.B.S. Lt –
"	18/1/18	Fri.	Fine mild day – Company paid out – Five reinforcements from Base taken on strength – Company training in morning – Strength of Coy 10 off. 171 OR –	A.B.S. Lt
"	19/1/18	Sat.	Fine, mild day – G.O.C. Division visited Coy in morning – Coy went to baths at HONDIGHEM – Inter section football competition proceeded with – No 3 Secn. 3 goals No 1 Secn 1 goal – Strength of Coy. 10 off. 171 OR – 2 Lt Hawes leave to U.K.	A.B.S. Lt.
"	20/1/18	Sun.	Fine day – Coy training in morning – Nos 1 & 2 Secns on range. Semi final inter Secn. football competition. H.Q. 3 goals Transport 2 goals – Strength of Coy. 9 off. 171 OR – Capt Foulds struck off strength –	A.B.S. Lt.
"	21/1/18	Mon.	Rain all day – Coy Training in billets. Strength of Coy: 9 off: 171 OR –	A.B.S. Lt –
"	22/1/18	Tues	Fine mild day – Coy Training – Football 147 MGC. 2 goals 147 T.M.B. 2 goals – Strength of Coy. 9 off 171 OR –	A.B.S. Lt
"	23/1/18	Wed.	Fine day – Coy. Training in morning – Final inter-section football cup. HQ 3 goals No 3 Secn 2 goals Strength of Coy – 10 off 175 OR – 2 Lt Watts (from Base) taken on strength & posted to No 2 Secn –	A.B.S. Lt
"	24/1/18	Thrs.	Fine day – Coy Training – Nos 3 & 4 Secns on range – Football officers & N.C.O's v Privates – Strength of Coy. 10 off 175 OR –	A.B.S. Lt.
"	25/1/18	Fri.	Fine day – Coy Training – Nos 1 & 2 Secns on range – Coy paid out – Strength of Coy – 10 off 175 OR A.B. Sellman Lieut 147 M.G. Coy.	A.B.S. Lt –

2353 Wt. W2544/1454 700,000 5/15 D. D. & L. A.D.S.S./Forms/C. 2118.

PAGE 31

Instructions regarding War Diaries and Intelligence Summaries are contained in F. S. Regs., Part II. and the Staff Manual respectively. Title pages will be prepared in manuscript.

Army Form C. 2118.

WAR DIARY of 147 MACHINE GUN COY -

~~or INTELLIGENCE SUMMARY.~~

(*Erase heading not required.*)

Place	Date	Day	Summary of Events and Information	Remarks and references to Appendices
CAESTRE AREA.	26/1/18	Sat	Fine day - Coy Training - R.U. Football match. Privates 2 tries, Officers + NCOs 1 try - Strength of Coy - 10 off 175 OR -	A.B.S. Lt
	27/1/18	Sun.	Foggy day - Coy to bathes at HONDIGHEM. Coy Training. Football 147 MGC 3 goals 254 MGC nil. Strength of Coy - 10 off 173 OR - Sgt Binns + Sgt Smoothy left for GRANTHAM.	A.B.S. Lt.
	28/1/18	Mon.	Fine day. Coy training in morning - Football in afternoon - O.C. Coy + 2nd C. to BRIGADE Conference in afternoon - Strength of Coy - 10 off. 173 OR -	A.B.S. Lt.
	29/1/18	Tues.	Fine day - Coy Training - Nos. 1 + 2 Secns. on range - Brigadier visited Company during morning - Football in afternoon (Scratch Sides) Strength of Coy 10 off 173 OR -	A.B.S. Lt
	30/1/18	Wed.	Coy Training - Barrage work + Coy drill - Football, Rugby (NU) 147 TMB 3 tries MG Coy 1 goal Strength of Coy - 10 off - 173 OR -	A.B.S. Lt

In the Field
31 - 1 - 18

A. B. Sillman Lieut.
147 M. G. Coy.

[illegible] Capt
Commdg 147 MG Coy

2353 Wt. W2544/1454 700,000 5/15 D. D. & L. A.D.S.S./Forms/C. 2118.

Vol 26

War Diary
of
147 Mach Gun Coy
for
February 1918

PAGE 32 –

Instructions regarding War Diaries and Intelligence Summaries are contained in F. S. Regs., Part II. and the Staff Manual respectively. Title pages will be prepared in manuscript.

WAR DIARY ~~or~~ of ~~INTELLIGENCE SUMMARY~~.

(Erase heading not required.)

147 MACHINE GUN COY –

Army Form C. 2118.

Place	Date	~~Hour~~ Day	Summary of Events and Information	Remarks and references to Appendices
CAESTRE AREA –	31/1/18	Thurs.	Coy Training – Tactical training in morning – GHENT race in afternoon. No 1 Secn. 1st No 2 Secn. 2nd No 3 Secn. 3rd No 4 Secn. 4th. Strength of Coy – 10 off 173 OR –	[signature]
	1/2/18	Fri	Hard frost – Coy training barrage work – Officers on Strength of Coy:— Capt J. Mubting MC. Comm Coy – Lt A.B. Sellman 2 in Command – 2Lt H. Smith OC No 1 Secn – Lt T Ward – OC No 2 Secn – 2Lt W. J. Watts. Sub Secn. off No 2 Secn. Lt H. Bacer OC No 3 Secn. 2Lt W.S Coates Sub Secn. off No 3 Secn – Capt M. F. Kinder OC No 4 Secn – 2nd Lt A. H. Clark Sub Secn. off. No 4 Secn – 2Lt W.A. Hawes Transport Officer – Strength of Coy 10 off 173 OR –	[signature]
	2/2/18	Sat.	Hard frost. Tactical Scheme in morning – Football 147 MGC v 254 MGC at CAESTRE 147 MGC. 4 goals 254 MGC 1 goal – Strength of Coy 10 off 173 OR –	[signature]
	3/2/18	Sun	Fine day – Coy Church Parade with 4th W.R.R. in morning –	[signature]
	4/2/18	Mon	Company training in the morning, in the afternoon football match v 4th Batt W.R.R. (A Coy) won by 5 goals to nil.	[signature]
	5/2/18	Tues	Fine day. Company left for MOULLE area at 9 A.M. Transport by road without incident of importance on route. Coy marched to EBBLINGHEM there entrained for WATTEN, detraining at 4 P.M. Thence by route march to MOULLE. Billeting completed by 7 P.M. A quiet day. Men very tired	[signature]
	6/2/18	Wed.	Coy on B range during day. Some good practice at 400–600x range.	

2353 Wt. W2544/1454 700,000 5/15 D. D. & L. A.D.S.S./Forms/C. 2118.

PAGE 33.—

Instructions regarding War Diaries and Intelligence Summaries are contained in F. S. Regs., Part II. and the Staff Manual respectively. Title pages will be prepared in manuscript.

WAR DIARY
or
~~INTELLIGENCE SUMMARY.~~
(Erase heading not required.)

147 MACHINE GUN COY

Army Form C. 2118.

Place	Date	~~Hour~~ Day	Summary of Events and Information	Remarks and references to Appendices
CAESTRE AREA			Long range fire control practice carried out, with excellent results. A quiet & uneventful day. Sick nil, Casualties Nil.	[illegible]
	7/2/18	Thurs.	A wet day, firing cancelled. Coy carried out training in billet area. A quiet day & night. Sick nil, casualties nil.	[illegible]
	8/2/18	Friday	A fine day, rather windy. Coy found range duties for Competition firing of Brigade. During the afternoon played 6th W.R.R. B coy in inter coy football competition. Lost 4-2. A good game. Quiet 24 hours. Sick Nil. Casualties Nil.	[illegible]
	9/2/18	Sat.	Coy took part in Battalion field firing on B Range. Very good practice carried out, especially in control of fire. Quiet uneventful 24 hours	[illegible]
	10/2/18	Sun	A fine day. Coy left MOULLE area, ~~[illegible]~~ en route for LEDERZELE Arrived 2 P.M. Men marched well. Sick nil, Casualties nil	[illegible]
	11/2/18	Mon	A fine day. Coy left LEDERZELE for CAESTRE by route march. Arrived at billets at 3 P.M. A long march. Men marched very well. Sick Nil Casualties nil.	[illegible]
	12/2/18	Tues	A fine day. Company engaged in cleaning up & overhauling after move. Sick nil casualties nil. A quiet uneventful 24 hours	[illegible]

2353 Wt. W2544/1454 700,000 5/15 D. D. & L. A.D.S.S./Forms/C. 2118.

PAGE 34

Instructions regarding War Diaries and Intelligence Summaries are contained in F. S. Regs., Part II. and the Staff Manual respectively. Title pages will be prepared in manuscript.

WAR DIARY
or
~~INTELLIGENCE SUMMARY.~~
(Erase heading not required.)

147 MACHINE GUN Coy.

Army Form C. 2118.

Place	Date	~~Hour~~ Day	Summary of Events and Information	Remarks and references to Appendices
	~~Feb 13~~ 13/2/18	Wed	A fine day. Company resumed training. Quiet & uneventful 24 hours Sick nil Casualties nil.	[illegible]
	14/2/18	Thurs	A fine day. Company carried on with training. Sick nil Casualties nil	[illegible]
	15/2/18	Friday	Bright frosty day. Company training in morning according to programme In the afternoon the company team played 4 Batt W.R. Regt. in Semi Final of football competition winning 4 goals to 3. Sick nil. Casualties nil.	[illegible]
	16/2/18	Sat	Bright frosty day with no wind Company training & recreation ~~throughout~~ the day according to programme. Lieut Sellman left Coy to go on Home establishment, Lieut Boxer appointed acting second in command.	[illegible]
	17/2/18	Sun	Frosty in the morning thawing later, but no wind. Company training proceeded with in morning, final of football competition in the afternoon the company being beaten by the 1/2 WR Field Ambulance by 3 goals to nil. Enemy aerial activity in the early part of the night, bombs being dropped near the billet area. Sick nil casualties nil.	[illegible]
	18/2/18	Mon	Bright Frosty day with no wind. Training as per programme. A quiet & uneventful 24 hours. Sick nil Casualties nil.	[illegible]
	19/2/18	Tues	Frosty in the morning with mist which cleared off by the afternoon 2/LT SMITH & LT WARD went up to reconnoitre the new line. Quiet 24 hours Sick nil Casualties nil Strength of Coy 10 Off 175 OR	G.J. Hallett

A5834 Wt. W4973/M687 750,000 8/16 D. D. & L. Ltd. Forms/C.2118/13.

PAGE 35

147th Machine Gun Company

Army Form C. 2118.

WAR DIARY
or
~~INTELLIGENCE~~ SUMMARY.

(Erase heading not required.)

Instructions regarding War Diaries and Intelligence Summaries are contained in F. S. Regs., Part II. and the Staff Manual respectively. Title pages will be prepared in manuscript.

Place	Date	~~Hour~~ DAY	Summary of Events and Information	Remarks and references to Appendices
	20/2/18	WED	Cold misty day slight fall of rain at midday. Preparation for move. Draft of 20 O.Rs arrived from Battalions to be transferred. 2/LT WATTS & 2/LT CLARKE & a party of 12 O.Rs proceeded as advance party to forward area. Sick nil Casualties nil Strength of Coy 10 Off & 196 O.R	C J Hall Lt
FORWARD AREA	21/2/18	THUR	Very fine mild day Company left CAESTRE AREA for Forward area by train at 2.30 pm arriving at CAFE BELGE via YPRES at 7 pm. A good move. Capt Nutting proceeded to join the 30th Div as second in Command of the M.G Battalion. LT H.S BOSER appointed acting C.O. LT W.J HALL MC appointed acting second in command. Casualties nil Sick 1 Strength of Coy 9 Off & 196 O.R	C J Hall Lt
	22/2/18	FRID	Wet & windy day. The C.O & 2 Section officers reconnoitred the new line all arrangements for coming relief completed. Casualties nil Sick 1 Strength of Coy 9 Off & 196 O.R	C J Hall Lt
	23/2/18	SAT	a fine day. The Company relieved the 2nd N.Z M.G Coy in Right Brigade Sector leaving HATAWAI Camp at 4.45 pm. Relief complete at 9.30 pm. A quiet & good relief. No 7 Gun heavily shelled about midnight one dud whizzbang entered dug out - no casualties. The S.O.S went up at 11.40 pm on Left Brigade front No 15 gun fired one belt on S.O.S line. Sick ~~nil~~ 1 Casualties nil Strength of Coy 9 off & 196 O R	C J Hall Lt
	24/2/18	SUN	A quiet fine day. The anti aircraft gun at No 11 position fired 30 rounds at enemy aircraft in afternoon. Nos 12 13 14 guns fired 2000 rds each on K1d11 K7a65 - K7a50 & J6d85. Enemy machine guns very active during night Sick ~~nil~~ 1 Casualties nil Strength of Coy 9 Off 196 O.R	C J Hall Lt

A5834 Wt. W4973/M687 750,000 8/16 D. D. & L. Ltd. Forms/C.2118/13

PAGE 36

Instructions regarding War Diaries and Intelligence Summaries are contained in F. S. Regs., Part II. and the Staff Manual respectively. Title pages will be prepared in manuscript.

WAR DIARY
or
~~INTELLIGENCE SUMMARY.~~
(Erase heading not required.)

147th Machine Gun Company — Army Form C. 2118.

Place	Date	~~Hour~~ DAY	Summary of Events and Information	Remarks and references to Appendices
	25/2/18	MON	A quiet day. Very wet in morning fine but windy later. Heavy shelling on front line. At 12.45 pm No 1 gun was hit & put out of action. Pte Garside of No 1 Section was killed & Pte Pearson wounded. Cpl Waddington & Pte Dobson & Hetty were sent to Rear HdQrs suffering from slight shell shock. At about 1.10 pm the bay next the alternative position was hit & knocked in. The shelling ceased at about 1.30 pm. Very good observation obtained from Centre Section HQ. On the whole a quiet day. Rations left Rear HQ at 2.30 am & arrived to time at the Ration Dump at 4 am. Casualties 2 Sick nil Strength of Coy 9 Off 193 O.R	Capt Hallett
	26/2/18	TUES	A fine day rather windy. A quiet 24 hours. Some enemy retaliation for Corps barrage which was put down at 4 am. It died away at about 5.5 am chiefly directly just in rear of front line with very little damage to front line. The front line was swept with machine gun fire between 10 pm & midnight. Two enemy aircraft flew along the front line at 6.45 am but were turned back by machine gun fire. Casualties 1 Sick nil Strength of Coy 9 Off 192 O.R	Capt Hallett
	27/2/18	WED	A fine day developing into a very wet & windy night. A quiet 24 hours. 3000 rounds were fired during the night on various targets. No 5 gun stood by during the night in anticipation of enemy attack but did not fire. The vicinity of No 2 gun heavily shelled from 1 pm to 2 pm ~~of~~ with high velocity 4.2 & 5.9 shells. The transport lines were moved to WACATOU CAMP ~~on~~ the move being complete at 3 pm. This makes the camp very compact WACATOU CAMP being one side of the road & MATAWAI CAMP the other. Casualties 1 Sick 1 Strength of Coy 9 Off 192 O.R	Capt Hallett

A5834 Wt. W4973/M687 750,000 8/16 D. D. & L. Ltd. Forms/C.2118/13.

www.ingramcontent.com/pod-product-compliance
Lightning Source LLC
Chambersburg PA
CBHW081408160426
43193CB00013B/2130
9781474527477